Collected Poems of Idris Davies

EDITED BY ISLWYN JENKINS

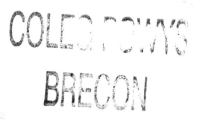

Collected Poems of
Idris Davies

GOMERIAN PRESS, LLANDYSUL

First Edition—June 1972
Second Edition—July 1980
Reprinted—January 1984
Reprinted—August 1990
Reprinted—October 1993

ISBN 0 85088 141 2

Printed in Wales
by J. D. Lewis & Sons Ltd., Gwasg Gomer, Llandysul

Acknowledgements

The editor and publishers wish to thank Mrs. Dorothy Morris, the poet's sister, for her kind permission to include published and unpublished work. Thanks are also due to Messrs. J. M. Dent & Sons Ltd., for permission to reprint *Gwalia Deserta* (1938) ; to Messrs. Faber for *The Angry Summer* (1943), *Tonypandy and Other Poems* (1945) and *Selected Poems* (1953) ; and to the editors of the following periodicals in which some of the poems first appeared : *Convoy, The Cornhill Magazine, Dock Leaves, Life and Letters Today, Merthyr Express, New English Weekly, Wales, The Welsh Review* and *Western Mail.*

This volume was commissioned by the Welsh Arts Council and is published with its financial support.

Contents

III   GLORY OUT OF CHAOS

Preface

No poet caught the drabness and warmth of life in the South Wales mining valleys during the troubled twenties and depressed thirties of this century as Idris Davies did. In his native Rhymney Valley in Monmouthshire, where he worked first as a miner and then finally as teacher and extra-mural lecturer in English literature, most of his poetic experience was centred and there, in 1953 at the age of forty-eight, he died of abdominal cancer. His literary friends in London knew him as troubadour of the black valley, and this association with an industrial valley in contrast with the vision of surrounding hills should be borne in mind if his poetry, which is essentially that of a personal Welsh-English border experience, is to be appreciated.

Attention so far, based on the four published volumes : *Gwalia Deserta* (Dent, 1938), *The Angry Summer* (Faber, 1943), *Tonypandy and other poems* (Faber, 1945) and *Selected Poems* (Faber, 1953), has stressed the social aspect of his work. Some influential critical accounts have pushed his work aside as propaganda poetry with designs upon its audience. Some who have praised him have done so in ways that reduce him to versifier of regional and passing interest. T. S. Eliot, who accepted three of the volumes for publication, considered that the work had permanence. W. B. Yeats expressed a wish to have the poem ' William Morris ' set to music. Dylan Thomas enjoyed public recital of the Bells poem from *Gwalia Deserta* and groups of young people in Britain and America appear to derive pleasure from its folktune. Little attention has yet been given to the poet's less political poems, especially those written after experience of Hitler's War had helped to modify his entire outlook. Some of this work, hidden away in magazines and journals or still in manuscript, has now become accessible. Now, for the first time, consideration of his poetic achievement as a whole and at each of its early, middle and late stages will be possible.

Because the work as a whole concerns direct experience and poetic observation the approach of this book is mainly biographical. The poems are grouped less according to subject-matter than to the poet's own formation and development. A strictly chronological arrangement could have been misleading because his constant search for poetic simplicity led to frequent revision even of already published work.

In the first section of the book an attempt is made to capture something of the poet's Welsh-speaking childhood and youthful experience among his native hills, the 'strange echoes' of a Celtic past in conflict with a post-calvinistic present which dominated his early environment. There is traditional Welsh awareness of mountains, moorland mists and curlews at dusk contrasted with growing consciousness of treeless scarred hillsides symbolising the vulgarity of economic greed through which individuals and communities of his industrial valley have been deprived of their birthright. A Welsh poem ' Cwm Rhymni ', selected from a number of early attempts to communicate in his first language, well illustrates this conflict : a dualism of mountain dream and coalmining reality ; its form resembling a Pantycelyn hymn, its content sharing the deceptive bitter-sweet simplicity of

Housman. ' Sonnet ', which concludes this first section of the book shows the tension objectified in an identity of artistic form with inner image.

The second section, ' bitter broken bread ', shows a poet socially and politically committed. *Gwalia Deserta* becomes the image of dry-bone mining valley life in the thirties when, after the dream and disaster of a General Strike in *The Angry Summer* of 1926, unemployed Welsh exiles went begging with broken hands in Babylonia. On visits to Sligo and Glasnevin the Welsh poet caught what he called ' Yeats' fever ' the effect of which appears in such poems as ' The Roses of the Sky ' : human decay in contrast with eternal beauty ; roses suffering with the poet and not merely as objects seen from a distance. At ' The Gate of Death ' during the war years 1939-1945 decay and beauty, transience and permanence became a terrifying matter of life and death. Several poems of this section reveal a humanist in difficulty seeking answers to the ' burthen of the mystery ' first in naturalism, then in an amoral faith in artistic beauty and finally in a universal compassion reflected in the long autobiographical poem ' I was born in Rhymney '.

The last section of the book, 'glory out of chaos', has a remarkable amount of Celtic Christian affirmation and shows the direction of the poet's development. There was movement away from propagandist political illusion towards a more realistic, simple sacramental materialism in which, as Professor Thomas shows in the Introduction, industrial valley life and mountain dream could become artistically one.

At each stage, therefore, and with varying degrees of intensity Idris Davies experienced tension which sought release. The fruit of the experience was a new entity which he accepted as a gift, which took shape and came to birth often after much suffering and hard work. His desire at each stage was communication, simple communication with other people whose aesthetic sensibilities he hoped to enrich.

ISLWYN JENKINS

Trinity College,
Carmarthen

Introduction

The small stature and vehement gestures of Idris Davies
concealed a powerful advocate and a withdrawn dreamer,
and the inner conflict between the Aristotelian poles of
rhetoric and poetics was never completely resolved in his
work. This collection of his verse will certainly help to
interpret his dual nature to a new generation of readers. It
is a difficult task, particularly for those of us who knew
him well and shared, without his painful understanding,
the breakdown of economic and social well-being that
occurred in the early industrial communities around the
source of the River Rhymney. Idris Davies was a man of
passionate conviction—Carlyle might have called him a
' Yea-sayer to life ' ; as a poet, this special quality of
affirmation often displays itself in excessive fluency. He
had so much to say, so many moods to share, and so many
moments of insight to communicate to others, that he
frequently allowed his urgency of statement to lie obscured
in unpolished stanzas, marred by easy rhymes and de-
vitalised by a nursery-rhyme-like rhythm. In this technical
sense he wrote too much too often ; the new reader should
not be put off by the resulting inelegance whenever it
occurs. For, in its totality, his verse makes a powerful,
individual statement (about the impact and outcome of the
decline of the Industrial Revolution in South Wales) that
can never be equalled or surpassed again. This side of his
verse seems to belong to the second kind of ' enthymemes '
(indicated by Aristotle) addressed to people who cannot
follow a train of reasoning, but who can be persuaded by
general arguments drawn from *topoi*, in its literal meaning
of the places in which arguments are to be found, the

regions, as it were, where they haunt. Consequently, at times, the verse may sound like a propagandist's jingle ; if so, this effect is not due to the bliss of literary ignorance. Idris Davies was far from unlettered : he was a self-educated poet who brought the bitter experience of life as miner, striker, and unemployed social discard, to his first acquaintance with the major English poets and with a few of the classical Welsh ones. His firsthand knowledge of poetry was immense and formed a major part of his life. The semi-autobiographical poem, *I was born in Rhymney*—the best introduction to his work—records the process tersely without extended comment :

> And I walked my native hillsides
> In sunshine and in rain,
> And learnt the poet's language
> To ease me of my pain.
>
> . . . . . .
>
> And I discovered Milton
> In a shabby little room
> Where I spent six summer evenings
> In most luxurious gloom.

This was in the period 1926-9 when he was studying for his ' matric.' by correspondence course. Later, in the winter of 1939-40, when, after first studying literature and history at Nottingham University College, then merging into part of the London Welsh literary scene, and, finally, publishing a volume of verse, Idris Davies demonstrates, in an entry in his unpublished diary, how free he was from contemporary literary fashion :

' I am a socialist. That is why I want as much beauty as possible in our everyday lives, and so am an enemy of pseudo-poetry and pseudo-art of all kinds. Too many "poets of the Left", as they call themselves, are badly in need of instruction as to the difference between poetry and propaganda. . . . These people should read Blake on Imagination till they show signs of understanding him. Then the air would be clear again, and the land be, if not full of, fit for song '.

One must emphasise the strong independence of his mind and judgement, for, superficially, he was a ' natural ' poet of the Left : he was a genuine proletarian writer—to use the jargon of the Thirties as I remember it so vividly—but he climbed on to no man's bandwaggon and his final decision to limit his topics was in answer to his own deepest needs as a poet. Further entries in his diary make this quite clear :

' I have met many kinds of escapists in my time. Perhaps the greatest escapists of all are fanatics, political and religious. How many extremists have I met in London and South Wales, young humourless people with a very slight or no regard for culture, but who blind themselves to the hard facts of everyday by their fanatical worship of theory ? These are the people who shout "Escape" when you talk of Spenser and Yeats. It is such people who depress and dishearten me when I think of the future.' (29 March 1940)

' Any subject which has not man at its core is anathema to me. The meanest tramp on the road is ten times more interesting than the loveliest garden in the world. And instead of getting nearer to nature in the countryside I find myself craving for more intense human society.' (19 February 1940)

These three quotations indicate the quality of his easy, familiar, unpublished prose ; they also suggest how selective the matter and the manner of his poetry was. A sophisticated student of literature, he chose a simple style for a special purpose—the need to speak for, and to, his own kind. To this extent the blurb on the jacket of *Gwalia Deserta* rings true. (' And their appeal is more than a literary one . . . one authorized by his people to sing for them, and to show the world in music what they have suffered and are still suffering in actuality '.) In the Thirties a great deal of poetry was remote from the ordinary reader. Idris Davies would have no truck with obscurity in poetry and deliberatively he seems to have adopted oversimplicity.

A brief selection from the poet's own statements in verse should make his intention quite plain :

> We have no frenzy in the heart,
> We play a mean mechanic part—
> You would not understand our way,
> Sweet singer of an idle day.
>
> (*William Morris*)

And in the ultimate autumn
The idiot and the horse
Shall sleep and dream for ever
Of man and all his wars.

(*Ultimate Autumn*)

From wandering in Worcester,
In Merthyr, and in Bow,
This is the truth I gather,
As naked as the snow :

The cur shall be in clover,
The poet in the sleet,
Till Christ comes into Dover
With fire at His feet—

(*Snowflake*)

Verily out of Gwalia
Shall come a soul on fire,
A prophet great in anger
And mighty in desire.

His words shall move the mountains
And make the floods rejoice,
And the people of his passion
Shall lift the golden voice.

(*Out of Gwalia*)

I love a voice that cracks the glass of life
And makes the whole world dim, most pale and dim
Against that sudden blaze of light
That flashes from the mind made swift
By the purged imagination.

> (From an unpublished verse play,
> *Beyond the Black Tips.* 1946)

Fame is the far-off and never dying legend
Of the artist's pride, and my pride
Is an old romantic ruin, mellow in September's sun.
My Lear shall carry his dead Cordelia to the edge of the
    world,
My Othello shall curse forever the midsummer moon,
My Falstaff be merry in ale on my funeral day,
My green Fool fool about with the ashes of my heart.

> (*The Retired Actor.* 10.iv.1951)

Make us, O Lord, a people fit for poetry.   (*Psalm*)

At first glance Idris Davies's published poetry seems to be
a denial of the spirit of these declared purposes. Their very
titles—*Gwalia Deserta* (1938), *The Angry Summer : A poem
of 1926* (1943), *Tonypandy and other poems* (1945)—offer
a circumscribed vision hemmed in by the stock Anglo-
Welsh properties of mining valley, pit-lamp, General
Strike, song, illicit passion, and neo-biblical hypocrisy.
And a hasty reading of the first two volumes would
confirm this impressionistic judgement. The following two

stanzas, taken from *Gwalia Deserta*, suggest parochial verse written at a level to be found only in the long-since defunct ' poetry columns ' of the *Merthyr Express* and the *Western Mail* :

> And they sold the fern and flower
> And the groves of pine
> For a hovel and a tankard,
> And the dregs are mine. (II)
>
> Though blighted be the valleys
> Where man meets man with pain,
> The things my boyhood cherished
> Stand firm, and shall remain. (XXXVI)

The poet, it seems, may urge others to adopt the Blakeian imagination, but the reader of Welsh hymnology and of some popular native poetry will not be surprised to find that the rhythm of these English verses echo Davies's own efforts at Welsh verse :

> Ar lannau Afon Rhymni
> Mi grwydrais lawer tro
> Pan nad oedd hwyl i ganu
> Ym mwg y pyllau glo.
>
> (*Cwm Rhymni*)
>
> Ei galon ef a ganodd
> Am bopeth ieuanc, iach,
> Ei nefoedd ef oedd heddwch
> Yng ngherddi'r pentre bach.
>
> (Ms. poem *Marwnad*)

Examining such poems of rudimentary design scattered throughout his published English verse, it would seem that when he is most personally involved in his chosen theme—industrialism as a kind of Welsh plague—Idris Davies echoes the rhythm of Welsh hymnology and Welsh poems of pastoral assent. If one were to ignore his prose statements, and the implied width of literary understanding behind them, one could make two crucial errors about his work : either, to confuse the poet's intention with his achievement, or, even worse error, to postulate the existence of some archetypal Anglo-Welsh subconscious stanza form that dominated the attempts of this Welsh-speaking, English-educated versifier to rise above the accents and structural sentence patterns of his early life. It is a mistake to confuse the poet as writer with the figure of the dreamer who moves in and out of his first two published volumes. Most of this verse was written while he was teaching in England, but he never lost his ear for the native dialect of his (and my) region. This dialect gives authentic strength to a 1937 notebook description of his accident as a miner :

' I looked at my hand and saw a piece of white bone shining like snow, and the flesh of the little finger all limp. The men supported me, and one ran for an ambulance box down the heading, and there was I fainting away like a little baby girl.'

He also wrote an unpublished novel, *Collier Boy*, based on his life as a miner and, in a preface added later, he wrote :

'Here you shall read a plain story, in straightforward English, of a boy who did not want to be a miner but who had to be one; who left the coalface for the teacher's desk, and who now wants to leave that for something else. . . . This book is not written to flatter the miner, or curse the mineowner, or to please or annoy any political gang. It is written to please myself . . . And for God's sake, don't search these pages for "literary style". I don't sell it.'

This preface is the most direct comment I know about his *Gwalia Deserta*.

After its favourable reception, Idris Davies considered a series of possible titles for a long poem : ' the 1926 strike, Oliver Cromwell, Napoleon, a mountain farm tragedy. I ought to settle down to it '. (Diary, 10 Jan. 1940). The final result was *The Angry Summer*, the purge of his own bitterness as a miner and striker, published with the accolade of Faber and Faber, together with the seal of T. S. Eliot's approval. The sequence was completed in three months and he confided to his diary : ' Poetry is composed of what you have seen and imagined and felt and wished and dreamed. You suddenly select the most vivid things out of all the wild forest of your mind '. Certainly, this faithfully reflects what he ' had seen and felt and wished ' ; provokingly it discounts so much of what he had ' imagined and dreamed '. For this reason, I believe, the deliberate restriction of topic was accompanied by a deliberate stylistic narrowing of range that is never completely offset by the skilful variation of tone and mood in each of the verse-sequences.

Like his friend Dylan Thomas, Davies was a perfervid admirer of Yeats and he understood the Irishman's claim that ' we make out of the quarrel with others, rhetoric, but of the quarrel with ourselves, poetry '. In time he learned to distinguish between the two quarrels. Although he died of gastric carcinoma before the process of separation was complete and never saw, although he would have understood, Yeats's (then) unpublished *General Introduction for my Work*, especially its opening sentence : ' A poet writes always of his personal life, in his finest work out of its tragedy, whatever it be, remorse, lost love, or mere loneliness : he never speaks directly as to someone at the breakfast table, there is always a phantasmagoria '. For Idris understood the role of the tragic sense in a poet's make-up. In December 1939 he felt that his poetry didn't flow because he hadn't suffered enough and, after reading Shaw, he records in his diary that ' perhaps Shaw has not suffered enough ; for it seems that the greatest art must have had intense agony as one of its chiefest impulses '. Yet, despite his penchant for the bold clarity of simple Blakeian statement—as in an early poem on *Poetry*, written in August 1933,

> Let it come as comes the rose
> To the summer tree,
> And to him who mostly knows
> Pain and ecstasy—

Idris Davies learned to disguise his easily triggered feelings and memories as a miner behind the masks of rhetorical attitudes and historical perspectives. In much of the verse in this present volume there is less direct correspondence between truth in his life and fiction in his verse than he would have us believe. In his own way he had come to terms with the problems posed for any writer by the ' cult of sincerity'. Many precise details in his autobiographical tour de force, *I was born in Rhymney*, are not strictly accurate ; he was thoroughly disillusioned with the Rhondda way of life, as he experienced it in the Second World War, despite much of the rhetoric of *Tonypandy* ; his lifelong assumption of a Deistic attitude to religion did not prevent his writing quite a few ' sincere ' carols. (There is the significant diary record on 24 December 1939, home in Rhymney for Christmas : ' Christianity, as we know it, is indubitably one of the weeds of human history. It must go. It will go. And yet, tomorrow morning, some time between breakfast and Christmas dinner, I will probably read again the second chapter of St. Luke for my childhood's sake ! ' Hoping it might be so ! ') It is no surprise then to read one of the last poems written before his final operation and illness in which he takes his own farewell to his craft in the guise of a retired actor. Idris Davies appreciated the need for a mask as readily as did Yeats or Dylan Thomas.

Where the critical doubt arises is between the poet's intention and its execution. There is no doubt in my mind that Idris—a warm, passionate and humorous man—took a conscious decision to write simple, impassioned verse like an Old Testament prophet, or a Greek orator, or a Welsh politician, in order to help make impossible in the future that murder and malformation of a society in the name of easy wealth which was how he saw the inception, growth, and final decay of the old iron-town of Rhymney. Adopting a prophetic stance—quite easy to do in the heyday of Welsh nonconformist preachers—he hoped to make live the dry bones of Welsh culture and even, as Hitler's war approached with the inevitability of Yeats's vision of the Second Coming, he half-hoped to stir the conscience of Britain as a whole. In a sense his poem on a *Socialist Victory* in 1945 echoes this pre-war vision, but by that time he had ceased to believe—if he ever had—in easy slogans. He knew the limits that divided propaganda from poetry and I believe that he adopted his typical quatrain, with all its dangers, not for ease of statement but because he hoped to reach a wider audience. His was a quest for a simpler kind of poetry than so many other poets practised in the 1930s. The final justification of this desire was the amazing *I was born in Rhymney* which, for me, is the complete justification of his dogged wish to write in a popular, public style. In a sense this poem almost supersedes *Gwalia Deserta* and *The Angry Summer*, as it certainly rendered unnecessary the poet's unpublished sequence *Out of Gwalia*.

Not all his poetry was of this familiar, pseudo-auto-biographical kind which reflects a wellknown South Walian habit of practised introspection and easy verbal ' confession '. Three elements in this complete volume of his verse should win readers for him beyond those who have already type-cast him, on the basis of his first three volumes, as a passionate, limited poet of social indignation. First of all, the surrounding poems in *Tonypandy* and the new poems in *Selected Poems* (published in 1953 just before his death) are now seen to be representative of a large number of poems (and attempted poems) of quite a different kind—more opaque in texture and more concerned with imaginations and dreams. Secondly, the tenacious hold over him of his childhood religious memories becomes much clearer, even though this mood is presented in so many of his inferior verses. Thirdly, the intensely concentrated effect of *Gwalia Deserta*, *The Angry Summer*, and *Selected Poems* seems to arise from the fact that they are not mere collections of isolated lyrics but are strictly conceived as long poems. There was a dramatic intention behind all his work, and some day it may be possible to publish a new selection of Idris Davies that gives adequate expression to this desire of his to perpetuate the memory of his Lear, his Othello, his Falstaff, and his green Fool.

In March 1940, after a long walk from Rhymney to Bedwellty Church and back, along one of the many ancient mountain ways that made life tolerable in the decaying mining valleys—particularly for unemployed miners and students—Idris Davies in an unpublished diary, reflected on his life :

'I felt very unsatisfied with my progress. I've spent eight of these years in London—from 1932 to 1939—and what have I done there, outside my daily work ? Nothing or very little. A few poems published here and there, a diploma in history, and a small book in 1938. No wife, no lectureship:

too shy to get the one ; too slow to get the other. So I mused rather sadly in the sunshine on the hills, on the hills of my childhood and youth, and yet I felt very happy coming home for late tea.'

Nothing could illustrate more clearly than this extract the dual nature of Idris Davies's poetry. Here is the determination, tinged with the ' writer's melancholy ', to achieve something, to make something of his life in a public way. Despite his satirical poems about *Capel Calvin*, this was an inevitable strand in his make-up. Ironically enough, this despised calvinistic drive urged him to write *Gwalia Deserta* and then, deliberately to purge himself of the bitter let-down of the 1926 Strike in *The Angry Summer* —that carefully arranged amalgam of lampoons, wistful-ness, satirical observation, and idealistic socialistic aspir-ation, which relies instinctively for its shape and tone on Housman and Hardy, the two poets he had discovered for himself in the early days of self-tuition immediately after the strike. But the diary entry also records a response to the hills of his childhood and youth. To me this is a direct link with much of nineteenth century Welsh poetry —especially the local poet, Islwyn—and that element in the nonconformist culture of my youth in the Rhymney Valley that somehow linked together an idyllic rural Wales of the past with the mountains and farms above the mining valleys and, subconsciously, with the Palestine of Christ's childhood. Two events shattered the cosy ambience of this hazy sentimental dream-world: the Great War and the 1926 Strike. (A third and less spectacular force, easy to see with hindsight, was the inevitable decay of the very early industrial systems that centred around Rhymney, Dowlais, and Tredegar.) To walk on these mountains, particularly from Rhymney—a kind of Clapham Junction for the old ways giving easy access to rural, industrial, and coastal Wales as well as to the English border counties—is to enter a timeless region which is everpresent in Idris Davies's verse, even in *The Angry Summer*.

He slowly learned to come to terms with this second side of his nature and a stream of poems, finished and half-finished as was his wont, testify to this process of resolution which was spread over his twenty years of writing verse. *Gwalia Deserta* XXIX is the most coherent early statement of this clash of mood in 'the dreamer in the mining town/ Who wandered in the evening to the hills . . .'

Wilder than the politician's yellow tongue
And stronger than the demagogue's thunder,
The insistent language of the dream would ring
Through the dear and secret places of the soul.
O fresher than the April torrent, the words of indignation
Would clothe themselves with beauty, and be heard
Among the far undying echoes of the world.

Similarly, although the penultimate lyric in *The Angry Summer* seems to end the sequence with truly militant finality,

But you will be sons of theirs,
Keeping their torches bright,

the final poem of the volume relates more closely to the experience of the dreamer on the hills, although he is a dreamer who has fought and lost alongside his comrades :

> The summer wanes, and the wine of words
> Departs with the departing birds.
> The roses are withering one by one
> And the lesser grasses grow sick of the sun,
>
> . . . . . .
> But the battle's end is not defeat
> To that dream that guided the broken feet
> And roused to beauty and to pride
> Toiler and toiler, side by side.

As so many of us can testify, this is less true than the reality of the gradual drift back to work, the recriminations, and the ' scabs '. The poem is not reportage : it partakes so much of the poet's own uncertain search for an ideal world to replace that lost one of his childhood that remained for him coherent and imaginatively complete. So he created his unreal world of miner-heroes

> Whose faith and courage shall be told
> In blaze of scarlet and of gold,

in his poem composed in the middle of the Second World War.

This is the questing spirit that informs poems like *In Dyfed, Permanence, Ruin, Ultimate Autumn, One February Evening, Interlude, Sonnet,* and *The Sacred Road* from

Tonypandy and other poems, and *Midnight, A Star in the East* and *Meesden in Hertfordshire* from *Selected Poems*, and then finally appears once more in a handful of manuscript verses —for example, *Mists upon the Sea* (1931) and *Dowlais Top* (1951)—that illustrate over twenty years the continuity of this one side of his temperament and achievement :

> For here I found the soul could sing whate'er the eye
> could see,
> Could sing about the beauty lost and the beauty yet to be,
> And probe to the impassioned thought that is the root of
> poetry.

The Retired Actor had come a long way in the understanding of self when he said

> For the blood of my life
> Was applause, applause of the fool and the sage,
> Of the mother and child.

Knowledge of the fundamental human relationships, both familial and social, is rarely absent from Idris Davies' poetry. Too often, like a minstrel, he strummed in verse in order to attract attention to his tale ; but sometimes he spoke quietly about himself and his dreams, and we are privileged to overhear his special blend of despair and rhetorical faith. Clarity of vision was his touchstone :

> If you will to Merthyr Tydfil,
> Ride unarmed of dreams;
>
> . . . . . .

> Pints of pity give no healing,
> Eyes go blind that will not see,
> Ride you into Merthyr Tydfil
> With salt of charity.

Yet the truth must be sustained by vision :

> The gods of great disasters
> May crack the hills tonight,
> But one man's dream is greater
> To build the world aright.

This was a faith that sustained Idris Davies as man and poet.

R. GEORGE THOMAS

Department of English,
University College of South Wales
*   and Monmouthshire,*
Cardiff.

I Strange Echoes

IN THE DUSK

When the mountains are grey in the evening
　　And cool are the winds from the west
And the lights in the valleys are twinkling
　　And the birds and the beasts go to rest,
I hear the strange echoes of armies
　　That glittered and conquered of old,
That marched to the beat of the ages
　　And lay down to sleep in the mould.

And I dream of the prince and the peasant
　　Who died for Glamorgan and Gwent,
And the Norman who scorned the Silurian
　　And ravaged the way that he went,
And the blood on the walls and the arches,
　　And the sweat of the toilers untold
Who toiled to the beat of the ages
　　And lay down to sleep in the mould.

1935 ; revised 1949

THE CURLEWS OF BLAEN RHYMNI

The curlews of Blaen Rhymni are calling in the night
And all the hills are magical because the moon is bright,
And I walk alone, and listen, along the mountain way
To curlew calling curlew in hollows far away.

And the crying of the curlew makes more sad and strange and fair
The moon above the moorland and the clear midnight air,
And the mountain breeze is laden with some echoes that must be
The echoes of a music beyond humanity.

And curlew calls to curlew, and I remember as I go
The merrier sounds and echoes out of seasons long ago,
When the nights were full of laughter and all the days were bright
And the heart too young to listen to the curlew in the night.

1945

RHYMNEY

(For Ceinfryn and Gwyn)

When April came to Rhymney
  With shower and sun and shower,
The green hills and the brown hills
  Could sport some simple flower,
And sweet it was to fancy
  That even the blackest mound
Was proud of its single daisy
  Rooted in bitter ground.

And old men would remember
  And young men would be vain,
And the hawthorn by the pithead
  Would blossom in the rain,
And the drabbest streets of evening,
  They had their magic hour,
When April came to Rhymney
  With shower and sun and shower.

MIDNIGHT

When the moon is full over Rhymney and the hillsides are
    silver-grey
And the old and the young are sleeping, and the scars of the
    common day
Are lost in the haze, I open the small window and stare
At the forms of the sleeping town, so still, so strangely fair.

Then I wonder if beauty demands that men must be put away
In graves and tombs before her profoundest peace can fill the
    night and day,
If all shall be perfect only when every town is under grass,
And nothing is left of our hearts and tongues after the loud
    years pass.

1935 ; revised 1947

WAUN FAIR

They sold apples and geese and ponies
In the fair upon the moor
On fine September mornings
Years and years ago.

They cursed and laughed and haggled
Until the deals were done,
And lifted pots of beer
Against the autumn sun.

And wily folk worked wonders
Upon the moor of old,
But the florins lasted longer
Than they who bought and sold.

And now the moor is silent,
With rougher winds to freeze
The lips of a Rhymney poet
Making bargains with the breeze.

FREE DISCIPLINE

I am the centre of all things and the world was made for me
For I am a pupil at a school where the discipline is free,
Where the masters are all crackers and the Head is out for fun
And the boy of greatest glory is the smartest with a pun.

My father and my mother, and my wealthy Aunty Dot,
They see my glorious future, and chat of it a lot,
And though they pay no visit, they believe in what they're told,
And praise the Annual Report, and shovel out the gold.

To sing about my studies would be awfully unfair,
For like that puss Macavity—the curriculum's not there,
So I sing a song of freedom, and wish all boys could be,
In Oxford or in Hoxton, as free of work as me.

For freedom is a noble thing, beloved from day to day,
When boys are free to pick and choose of either work or play
And free to tell their masters when to stop or when to start,
And free to yell with raucous throat what feels the boyish heart.

O we shall cherish Freedom—you can bet your shirt on that—
Till our masters are our errand boys, and the Head is on the mat,
For we at least have wit enough to see where Folly rules
And how to reap advantage when we meet with cranks and fools.

1946

CWM RHYMNI

Ar lannau Afon Rhymni
Mi grwydrais lawer tro
Pan nad oedd hwyl i ganu
Ym mwg y pyllau glo.

Ar lethrau llwyd Cwm Rhymni,
Yn oriau'r gwynt a'r glaw,
Trist oeddwn yn breuddwydio
Am ryw binaclau draw.

Pinaclau'r oesoedd euraidd
Tu hwnt i'r dydd a'r nos,
Breuddwydion ffôl y galon
A'u gwreiddiau yn y rhos.

Ond 'nawr, ple bynnag crwydraf,
Mae miwsig yn fy ngho'
Am fachgen yn breuddwydio
Ym mwg y pyllau glo.

(In this simple, traditional Welsh lyric about the Rhymney Valley
there is recollection of many wanderings along the banks of the
Rhymney River when, beclouded by industrial smoke, the poet had
no inspiration for song : on grey slopes of the valley in hours of wind
and rain his sad dreaming of distant summits, golden-age peaks beyond
day and night ; the heart's foolish dreams with roots in the moorland.
But now, wander where he will, memory recalls music of a boy
dreaming in spite of coal-pit smoke.)

CAPEL CALVIN

There's holy holy people
They are in capel bach—
They don't like surpliced choirs,
They don't like Sospan Fach.

They don't like Sunday concerts,
Or women playing ball,
They don't like Williams Parry much
Or Shakespeare at all.

They don't like beer or bishops,
Or pictures without texts,
They don't like any other
Of the nonconformist sects.

And when they go to Heaven
They won't like that too well,
For the music will be sweeter
Than the music played in Hell.

DEACON AT BETHANY

' Ghost with the bowler hat
Under the sycamore tree,
Why do you laugh like that
And laugh so long at me ? '

' O pious public man,
Deacon at Bethany,
Be solemn as long as you can
Before you dance with me.

' For with me under the boughs
You'll rattle your bones in glee
At the way you walked from your house
To the chapel after tea.

' And your hat will be on your head
In comic memory
Of the things you did and said
In the chapel called Bethany '.

THE LAY PREACHER PONDERS

' Isn't the violet a dear little flower ? And the daisy, too.
What nice little thoughts arise from a daisy !
If I were a poet now—but no, not a poet,
For a poet is a wild and blasphemous man ;
He talks about wine and women too much for me
And he makes mad songs about old pagans, look you.
Poets are dangerous men to have in chapel,
And it is bad enough in chapel as it is
With all the quarrelling over the organ and the deacons ;
The deacons are not too nice to saintly young men like me.
(Look at Jenkin John Jones, the old damn scoundrel !)
They know I can pray for hours and hours,
They know what a righteous young man I am,
They know how my Bible is always in my pocket
And Abraham and Jonah like brothers to me,
But they prefer the proper preacher with his collar turned round ;
They say he is more cultured than I am,
And what is culture but palaver and swank ?
I turn up my nose at culture.
I stand up for faith, and very simple faith,
And knowledge I hate because it is poison.
Think of this devilish thing they call science,
It is Satan's new trick to poison men's minds.
When I shall be local councillor and a famous man—
I look forward to the day when I shall be mayor—
I will put my foot down on clever palaver,
And show what a righteous young man I am.
And they ought to know I am that already,
For I give all my spare cash to the chapel
And all my spare time to God. '

THE BALLAD OF A BOUNDER

He addressed great congregations
  And rolled his tongue with grease,
And his belly always flourished,
  In time of war or peace.

He would talk of distant comrades
  And brothers o'er the sea,
And snarl above his liquor
  About neighbours two or three.

He knew a lot about public money—
  More than he liked to say—
And sometimes sat with the paupers
  To increase his Extra pay.

He could quote from Martin Tupper
  And Wilhelmina Stitch,
And creep from chapel to bargain
  With the likeliest local bitch.

He could swindle and squeal and snivel
  And cheat and chant and pray,
And retreat like a famous general
  When Truth would bar his way.

But God grew sick and tired
  Of such a godly soul,
And sent down Death to gather
  His body to a hole.

But before he died, the Bounder
   Said : ' My children, be at peace ;
I know *I* am going to heaven,
   So rub my tongue with grease.'

SONG

They tried in a Primitive Chapel
To teach his soul to be sad,
To make him blind to the body
And the joys the body had,
O the joys the body had !

They assumed he would end as a deacon
To sigh and wail and moan,
To be one of a stout black dozen
Who tune their tongues to a groan,
O tongues all tuned to a groan !

But lo, he met with Rabelais
One day in a sunlit room,
And he vowed to feast with Rabelais
Until the day of doom,
O the distant day of doom !

COME TO OUR REVIVAL MEETING

And this is the sordid dream of the drunkard creeping to prayer,
And the maddened mob drowning the noise of the birds
Frightened and fluttering in the dusty trees,
And all the hysterical converts insulting the heavens,
The brown pond sticky with the thighs of the damned ;
And here comes a fellow to shake your liver
For out of his nightmare he leapt
When the moon crept up behind the Iron Bridge
And the garbage heap, where the trollop sat waiting
To sell her filth to the fool. And I saw
All this shabby mockery of April
As a neurotic's delirium, his hallucination
Of apes and angels and dog-headed ghosts
Mingling and whirling and circling and dancing
Among the decaying boughs that laced like serpents
The ripped edges of the darkening sky.

O Lord God, save us from tinned donkey,
From Soviet scientific magazines,
From the Scottish Sabbath, from American war films,
From the demagogues of Aberdare and Abadan,
And above all, O Lord God, save us from the Pentecostals.

RENAISSANCE

The cocks of the south were crowing,
  And white sails shone on the sea,
And Rabelais rolled with laughter
  Under the richest tree.

Leonardo da Vinci pondered
  On the fat cheeks of mine host,
And Shakespeare whispered to Webster
  Of maids who pressed the most.

Kit Marlowe reached to the branches
  Where the golden apples grow,
And marble felt the fury
  of Michelangelo.

O the sons of the west were singing
  And the skies of the west were fair,
And poet and painter and pirate
  Struck treasure everywhere.

Glory of sound and colour,
  Glamour of women and wine,
And the masters of music celestial
  Found the dust of the earth divine.

1937

THE HEART OF A DREAMER

I broke my heart in five pieces
And buried a part by the sea,
And I hid a part in the mountains
And the third in the root of a tree,
And the fourth I gave to a singer
Who shared his wild ecstasy,
But the best I gave to a woman
Who gave all her heart to me.

LOVE LASTS LONGER

Love lasts longer than the roses,
Love is warmer than the wine,
Love is wilder than the whirlwind,
    And O that love were mine !

Love is older than the mountains,
Love is fresher than the tides,
Love is sweeter than the lilies,
    And O that love were mine !

Love is stronger than the granite,
Love is gentler than a sigh,
Love is richer than the rubies,
    And O that love were mine !

Love lasts longer than the roses,
    And O that love were mine . . .

1937

SONNET

I tossed my golden anchor to the sea
To tease the twisted tides of salty joy,
And then my heart pursued the mystery
Of sea-born kings that did the moon annoy
Before the horn of summer caught the tune
Born in the shell of grief. The velvet bone
Of sea-weed forests melted in the noon
And every frond bent down to clasp the stone.
Sea-bottom surge, be gentle with my bread
For in my bread there sleeps another god
Whose hands are clean, whose heart is strong and red;
The idols of old Sabbaths loved the rod
And smiled to see our blood on window panes
And danced upon the dead in thistled lanes.

1937

II Bitter Broken Bread

THE VICTIMS

In that long and crooked valley
the father and the son
were crucified together
against a garish sun.

Their graves are ever frowning,
so grim and vast are they,
on the poisoned and the crippled
creatures of the day.

And sunset and her shadow
bequeath the riddled dead
the token everlasting
of bitter, broken bread.

A VICTORIAN PORTRAIT

You stood behind your Bible
And thundered lie on lie,
And your roaring shook your beard
And the brow above your eye.

There was squalor all around you
And disaster far ahead,
And you roared the fall of Adam
To the dying and the dead.

You built your slums, and fastened
Your hand upon your heart
And warned the drab illiterate
Against all useless art.

And you died upon the Sabbath
In bitterness and gloom,
And your lies were all repeated
Above your gaudy tomb.

THE SACRED ROAD

They walked this road in seasons past
When all the skies were overcast,
They breathed defiance as they went
Along these troubled hills of Gwent.

They talked of justice as they strode
Along this crooked mountain road,
And dared the little lords of Hell
So that the future should be well.

Because they did not count the cost
But battled on when all seemed lost,
This empty ragged road shall be
Always a sacred road to me.

MARX AND HEINE AND DOWLAIS

I used to go to St. John's Wood
On Saturday evenings in summer
To look on London behind the dusty garden trees,
And argue pleasantly and bitterly
About Marx and Heine, the iron brain and the laughing sword;
And the ghost of Keats would sit in a corner,
Smiling slowly behind a summer of wine,
Sadly smiling at the fires of the future.
And late in the summer night
I heard the tall Victorian critics snapping
Grim grey fingers at London Transport,
And sober, solemn students of James Joyce,
Dawdling and hissing into Camden Town.

But now in the winter dusk
I go to Dowlais Top
And stand by the railway bridge
Which joins the bleak brown hills,
And gaze at the streets of Dowlais
Lop-sided on the steep dark slope,
A battered bucket on a broken hill,
And see the rigid phrases of Marx
Bold and black against the steel-grey west,
Riveted along the sullen skies.
And as for Heine, I look on the rough
Bleak, colourless hills around,
Naked and hard as flint,
Romance in a rough chemise.

COME DOWN

Come down, young mountain dreamer, to the crowded public
    square
Where anger breaks into music and thrills through the common
    air,
And leave to fade behind you the fantasies you fed
From the sentimental sluices of a culture dying and dead.

Come down from the mindless mountain and let your day
    dreams die
On the aimless wind that wanders across the friendless sky,
And come with your senses quickened and give of the best you
    can
To speed the day that knows anew the dignity of man.

OUT OF GWALIA

Verily out of Gwalia
   Shall come a soul on fire,
A prophet great in anger
   And mighty in desire.

His words shall move the mountains
   And make the floods rejoice,
And the people of his passion
   Shall lift the golden voice.

A prophet out of Gwalia
   Shall rouse the heart again,
Give courage to the bosom
   And beauty to the brain.

GWALIA DESERTA

I

The Commissioners depart with all their papers
And the pit-heads grin in the evening rain ;
The white deacons dream of Gilead in the Methodist vestry
And the unemployed stare at the winter trees.
The parallel valleys crawl to the Severn shore,
And adolescents jazz in the mining village,
And somebody's only daughter is in trouble.
The Sabbath choristers in Bethel praise the Lord ;
And young men at street-corners are aimless and ragged,
And the old, old miners sit and dream
Of the mirth and the pain of the distant years.

II

My fathers in the mining valleys
    Were slaves who bled for beer,
Who had no Saviour to acclaim
    And whose god was Fear.

And they sold the fern and flower
    And the groves of pine
For a hovel and a tankard,
    And the dregs are mine.

So in these rain-swept graveyards
    Where my fathers sleep,
Shall I sulk, and curse them
    Who made their lives so cheap ?

[*Gwalia Deserta*

Or shall I pause, and pity
    Those luckless lads of old,
Those sullen slaves whipped onward
    To load my lords with gold ?

Bute

III

In Cardiff at dawn the sky is moist and grey
And the baronets wake from dreams of commerce,
With commercial Spanish grammar on their tongues ;
And the west wind blows from the sorrowful seas,
Carrying Brazilian and French and Egyptian orders,
Echoing the accents of commercial success,
And shaking the tugs in the quay.
Puff, little engine, to the valleys at daybreak,
To northward and westward with a voice in the dawn,
And shout to the people that prosperity's coming,
And that coal can be changed into ingots of gold,
And that Cardiff shall be famous when the sun goes down.

Pit Props.

IV

O timbers from Norway and muscles from Wales,
Be ready for another shift and believe in co-operation,
Though pit-wheels are frowning at old misfortunes
And girders remember disasters of old ;
O what is man that coal should be so careless of him,
And what is coal that so much blood should be upon it ?

Gwalia Deserta]

27

V

He is digging in the dark,
  Jude who would the poet be,
And dreaming of the distant isles
  And the summer on the sea.

Not for always shall he grope
  In the galleries of grime—
'Tis sure he shall be shouldered,
  And need nor pick nor rhyme.

VI

Down from your shining mountains,
Dreamers of glory to be,
Back to your derelict valleys,
Back to your slums by the sea.
Back to your little parsons
And all their pious tales,
Back to your brawny demagogues
Whose fervour never fails !

Dream no more on your mountains
But face the savage truths
That snarl and yell in your valleys
Around your maids and youths.
Down from your dreams in the mountains,
Back to your derelict mate,
For the dreamers of dreams are traitors
When wolves are at the gate.

VII

There are countless tons of rock above his head,
And gases wait in secret corners for a spark ;
And his lamp shows dimly in the dust.
His leather belt is warm and moist with sweat,
And he crouches against the hanging coal,
And the pick swings to and fro,
And many beads of salty sweat play about his lips
And trickle down the blackened skin
To the hairy tangle on the chest.
The rats squeak and scamper among the unused props,
And the fungus waxes strong.

And Dai pauses and wipes his sticky brow,
And suddenly wonders if his baby
Shall grow up to crawl in the local Hell,
And if to-morrow's ticket will buy enough food for six days,
And for the Sabbath created for pulpits and bowler hats,
When the under-manager cleans a dirty tongue
And walks with the curate's maiden aunt to church . . .

Again the pick resumes the swing of toil,
And Dai forgets the world where merchants walk in morning
     streets,
And where the great sun smiles on pithead and pub and
     church-steeple.

VIII

Do you remember 1926 ? That summer of soups and speeches,
The sunlight on the idle wheels and the deserted crossings,
And the laughter and the cursing in the moonlit streets ?
Do you remember 1926 ? The slogans and the penny concerts,
The jazz-bands and the moorland picnics,
And the slanderous tongues of famous cities ?
Do you remember 1926 ? The great dream and the swift
    disaster,
The fanatic and the traitor, and more than all,
The bravery of the simple, faithful folk ?
' Ay, ay, we remember 1926, ' said Dai and Shinkin,
As they stood on the kerb in Charing Cross Road,
' And we shall remember 1926 until our blood is dry. '

IX

When greed was born
In Monmouthshire,
The hills were torn
For Mammon's fire,
And wheels went round
And skulls were cracked,
And limbs were ground
And nerves were wracked.
No time to dream,
No time to stare,
In that fell scheme
To foul the air,
To grab the coal
And scorn the tree,

[*Gwalia Deserta*

And sell the soul
To buy a spree.
And breasts were bruised
In dismal dens,
And streets were used
As breeding pens,
And babes were born
To feed the fire,
When hills were torn
In Monmouthshire.

X

Down the river in the morning flow the empty corn-beef
tins,
Down the river in the evening flow the curses of the crowd,
Down the river in the midnight flow the little broken dreams,
Down the river through the seasons flow the dregs of all our
griefs.
O little crooked shabby river hurrying down to Severn Sea,
Tell the ships of all the oceans of the tragic towns you know,
Of the aimless, hopeless mornings and the patient men who
wait
In the streets and on the ridges, in the sun and in the snow.

XI

Dark gods of all our days,
　Have mercy upon us.

Dark gods, take away
　The shadows from our towns,

The hopeless streets, the hovels
　Behind the colliery sidings.

Dark gods of grime and grief,
　Soften the bitter day,

And give our children eyes
　To see somewhere a summer.

Dark gods, we beg you,
　Make us proud and angry,

That we shall rise from shame
　And imitate the torrent,

And scatter the high priests
　Who deal in blood and gold.

Dark gods of all our days,
　Dark gods of life and death,

Have mercy upon us
　Who wait in the shadow.

[*Gwalia Deserta*

XII

There's a concert in the village to buy us boots and bread,
There's a service in the chapel to make us meek and mild,
And in the valley town the draper's shop is shut.
The brown dogs snap at the stranger in silk,
And the winter ponies nose the buckets in the street.
The ' Miners' Arms ' is quiet, the barman half afraid,
And the heroes of newspaper columns on explosion day
Are nearly tired of being proud.
But the widow on the hillside remembers a bitterer day,
The rap at the door and the corpse and the crowd,
And the parson's powerless words.
And her daughters are in London serving dinner to my lord,
And her single son, so quiet, broods on his luck in the queue.

XIII

The northern slopes are clouded
    And Rhymney streets are wet,
The winds sweep down from the mountains
    And night has cast her net.

The ghosts of a thousand miners
    Walk back to the streets again,
And the winds wail in the darkness,
    And Rhymney sighs in the rain.

XIV

Roaming the derelict valley at dusk,
Breathing the air of desolation,
Watching the thin moon rise behind the mountain church,
I seek in the faces of men glimpses of early joy,
I seek in the sounds of human speech
The echoes of some far forgotten rapture. . . .
Alas, the wind from the moor squeaks through deserted
    machinery,
And pulls at the edges of tawdry advertisements,
Shakes patched-up shirts and drawers on backyard lines,
Shakes the last brown leaves on the hawthorn hedge ;
And many eyes are fixed on ' our expert tipster '.

XV

O what can you give me ?
Say the sad bells of Rhymney.

Is there hope for the future ?
Cry the brown bells of Merthyr.

Who made the mineowner ?
Say the black bells of Rhondda.

And who robbed the miner ?
Cry the grim bells of Blaina.

They will plunder willy-nilly,
Say the bells of Caerphilly.

They have fangs, they have teeth !
Shout the loud bells of Neath.

34

To the south, things are sullen,
Say the pink bells of Brecon.

Even God is uneasy,
Say the moist bells of Swansea.

Put the vandals in court !
Cry the bells of Newport.

All would be well if—if—if—
Say the green bells of Cardiff.

Why so worried, sisters, why ?
Sing the silver bells of Wye.

XVI

We went to Cardiff when the skies were blue
And spent our shillings freely
In Queen Street and the bright arcades,
And in the cockle market.
And dainty little typists and daintier little gentlemen
Smiled most scornfully upon our cruder accents.
But we were happy unambitious men
Ready to laugh and drink and forget,
And to accept the rough and ready morrows
Of the mining valleys.
We tasted strawberries and cream,
And perhaps we thought our transient luck would last,
And perhaps we dreamed a little in Cathays,

Gwalia Deserta]

35

And we crowded into cinemas and cafés,
Or danced at evening, or sought a burning wench
And told her many tales.

And in the night, we laughed our way back home again
In trains that whistled merrily.
And some would open carriage windows
And gaze upon the stars above the Severn plain,
And some would jest about a woman,
And some would slip into a perfect sleep.

Back in our homes, by flickering fires,
We bade the day farewell in careless language,
And sought the simple beds of happy men.

XVII

It is bitter to know that history
Fails to teach the present to be better than the past,
For man was a slave in the morning of time
And a slave he remains to the last.

Once he crawled in the barbarous gloom
As the trembling slave of theology,
And to-day he moves in his sweat and his tears
As the servile fool of machinery.

It is bitter to know that all his dreams
Are roses that die to nourish the weeds,
That murder and malice and pain and grief
Are the surest traces of all his deeds.

[*Gwalia Deserta*

XVIII

Play dominoes till dusk, play dominoes and sigh,
For who will give you work again ?
Your fists are growing tender with the years,
And all the April hopes you had
Are lifeless leaves in autumn gutters.
So call your cronies to that table by the stove
In the little Welfare Institute,
And play and talk until the valley lights are lit.
Gaze out through dusty window panes
On delicate parsons passing by,
And the children of Gwalia seeking soup.
Or call to your side some veteran, grey and scarred,
And listen to the anecdotes of Chartism
That the veteran's father told,
And listen, listen to the frantic footsteps of the past
When the red-coats rode to Gwalia to beat the toilers down.
But if the sun is on the valley sides,
Go lie among the hillside fern, forgetting all the gangs,
And gaze upon those distant paths of boyhood,
And praise again the glory of the mountain grass,
And love again those mountain meres and those shepherds'
    walls.
Do you remember, as you lie among the fern,
The Sunday School, the coal-face, and the girl who teased
    you first ?
The football that you played among the coal-tips in the
    evening,
The lads you laughed with on your way from work ?
The times you sang with Dai in the local eisteddfod,
With Dai and Glyn and Emrys, singing the songs of Zion,
Of Gilead and of Galilee ?

Gwalia Deserta]

XIX

We have fooled ourselves that a Heaven
Awaits our bodiless selves
Or built out of fear a savage Hell
Of eternally flaming shelves.

And we raise our far Eldorados
In invisible valleys of air
While we crawl 'twixt the pub and the chapel,
Chewing the cud of despair.

XX

O where are our fathers, O brothers of mine ?
By the graves of *their* fathers, or awaiting a sign.
The Welsh skies are sullen, and the stars are all dim,
And the dragon of Glyndwr is bruised in the limb.
The brown earth is waiting for brothers of mine
And our mothers are hanging the shrouds on the line.
The deacons are groaning and the sheep-dogs are thin
And Dai is in London drinking tea from a tin.

XXI

I hear you calling on the mountains,
    Poet of the promised day,
I hear you from this stricken township,
    Calling far away.

I hear you calling in the twilight,
    A trumpet that shall be
To stir the towns and cities
    Along the Severn Sea.

38

XXII

I stood in the ruins of Dowlais
And sighed for the lovers destroyed
And the landscape of Gwalia stained for all time
By the bloody hands of progress.
I saw the ghosts of the slaves of The Successful **Century**
Marching on the ridges of the sunset
And wandering among derelict furnaces,
And they had not forgotten their humiliation,
For their mouths were full of curses.
And I cried aloud, O what shall I do for my fathers
And the land of my fathers ?
But they cursed and cursed and would not answer
For they could not forget their humiliation.

XXIII

In Gwalia, in my Gwalia,
   The vandals out of Hell
Ransacked and marred for ever
   The wooded hill and dell.

They grabbed and bruised and plundered
   Because their greed was great,
And slunk away and purchased
   The medals of the State.

XXIV

Because I was sceptical in our Sunday School
And tried to picture Jesus crawling in the local mine,
The dozen deacons bred on the milk of Spurgeon
Told me I was dangerous and in danger,
That I would be roasted and pronged and tossed like a pancake;
And then they would frown and go apart to pray.
On Sabbath evenings when I yawned in grandmother's pew,
When the parson roused himself with his raised arms,
And the elders cried out ' Amen, Amen ',
And Jenkins the Joiner nudged his wife with a caramel,
And tired mothers were musing on carpets and insurance
    agents,
And young fathers coaxed tiny boys to sleep,
I remember I used to stare through the chapel windows
Watching the sun like a perfect tomato touching the hill,
And a swarthy young man wandering on a purple ridge,
And his body was bent and his smile was compassionate.
And sometimes in mid-week I would see him again,
And we would smile and understand.

XXV

Who seeks another kingdom
Beyond the common sky ?
Who seeks the crystal towers
That made the martyrs sigh ?

On earth alone your towers,
By human strength, shall stand,
And the waters of your mountains
Alone shall save the land.

[*Gwalia Deserta*

Your cities shall be founded
On human pride and pain,
And the fire of your vision
Shall clean the earth again.

XXVI

The village of Fochriw grunts among the higher hills ;
The dwellings of miners and pigeons and pigs
Cluster around the little grey war memorial.
The sun brings glitter to the long street roofs
And the crawling promontories of slag,
The sun makes the pitwheels to shine,
And praise be to the sun, the great unselfish sun,
The sun that shone on Plato's shoulders,
That dazzles with light the Taj Mahal.
The same sun shone on the first mineowner,
On the vigorous builder of this brown village,
And praise be to the impartial sun.
He had no hand in the bruising of valleys,
He had no line in the vigorous builder's plans,
He had no voice in the fixing of wages,
He was the blameless one.
And he smiles on the village this morning,
He smiles on the far-off grave of the vigorous builder,
On the ivied mansion of the first mineowner,
On the pigeon lofts and the Labour Exchange,
And he smiles as only the innocent can.

XXVII

So we're all Welsh boys gathered together,
Boys bach, boys bach,
We have roamed from the rain and the ruins,
Boys bach, boys bach.

We have come with the songs of our fathers
And our mothers' tears,
We have come from the shores of the Severn,
Out of the sorrowful years.

We have lingered with Tydfil the tragic,
Boys bach, boys bach,
We have dreamed of the days of Pendragon,
Boys bach, boys bach.

And we come to the gates of Londinium,
Begging with broken hands,
Boys bach, boys bach all together,
Out of the derelict lands.

XXVIII

O dreary township in the hills !
The damp streets under the mountain,
Ragged children on broken pavements,
Young men sitting on cemetery walls,
Young girls dreaming of London ;
Old men remembering by fading fires,
Remembering Gladstone and Victoria and Mafeking ;

Grey mothers sighing by the windows,
Half-listening to Jenkin's speckled cockerel crowing on the
    tip ;
A funeral cortège creeping to the bleakest ridge
And the melancholy echoes of the chaunted hymns.
Yet sometimes in the night there is beauty
When the lights in the valley brag to the stars,
Or the moon of the moorland smiles on desolation.

XXIX

There was a dreamer in the mining town
Who wandered in the evening to the hills
To lie among grass, and gaze until the day
Had faded into night.
And good it was to breathe the mountain air,
The clean, sweet mountain air, and listen
To a hundred larks make song above the world ;
To see the grasses shine and stir and sway,
And watch the blue mists gather in the south ;
To smell the mountain herbs at dusk. . . .
O fine it was to be alive and young
And feel the beauty of the summer hills,
To lose the puny self, forget the drab
And heavy toil beneath the massy earth.

There in the dusk the dreamer dreamed
Of shining lands, and love unhampered
By the callous economics of a world
Whose god is Mammon.

Gwalia Deserta]

There in the mountain dusk the dream was born,
The spirit fired, and the calm disturbed
By the just anger of the blood.
Wilder than the politician's yellow tongue
And stronger than the demagogue's thunder,
The insistent language of the dream would ring
Through the dear and secret places of the soul.
O fresher than the April torrent, the words of indignation
Would clothe themselves with beauty, and be heard
Among the far undying echoes of the world.

And slowly the west would lose its crimson curves,
The larks descend, the hidden plover cry,
And the vast night would darken all the hills.

XXX

Ride you into Merthyr Tydfil
Where the fountains have run dry,
And gaze upon the sands of fortune
But pray not to the sky.

If you will to Merthyr Tydfil,
Ride unarmed of dreams ;
No manna falls on Merthyr Tydfil,
And there flow no streams.

Pints of pity give no healing,
Eyes go blind that will not see,
Ride you into Merthyr Tydfil
With salt of charity.

[*Gwalia Deserta*

No faith

XXXI

Consider famous men, Dai bach, consider famous men,
All their slogans, all their deeds,
And follow the funerals to the grave.
Consider the charlatans, the shepherds of the sheep !
Consider the grease upon the tongue, the hunger of the purse !
Consider the fury of the easy words,
The vulgarity behind the brass,
The dirty hands that shook the air, that stained the sky !

Yet some there were who lived for you,
Who lay to die remembering you.

Mabon was your champion once upon a time
And his portrait's on the milk-jug yet.
The world has bred no champions for a long time now,
Except the boxing, tennis, golf, and Fascist kind,
And the kind that democracy breeds and feeds for Harringay.
And perhaps the world has grown too bitter or too wise
To breed a prophet or a poet ever again.

XXXII

Ten million stars are burning
   Above the plains to-night,
But one man's dream is greater
   To set the world alight.

The gods of great disasters
   May crack the hills to-night,
But one man's dream is greater
   To build the world aright.

Gwalia Deserta]

XXXIII

The township in the twilight is quiet and sad and grey ;
In the valley, one after one the little yellow lights appear,
And on the rain-washed platform the young man says goodbye.
Mile after curving mile, the valley towns are dim and dumb,
The river shines and frets, and turns abruptly east,
The stars are high above the smooth green plain,
The smug green belt between the coalfield and the sea.
You gaze upon the fashionable suburb of Cardiff
And you smile and remember the post-war boom, the Sankey
    Award,
The Saturday afternoons specially made for Cardiff City,
The avalanche of hands and feet to Ninian Park,
The clamour and the roar, disputed goal, play up the blues,
The brass band at half-time, *Abide with Me*, and *Sospan Fach*,
The pigeons released and sweeping north and east and west,
The beer bottles waving, the mascot vendors,
And then the returning crowd, the great hoarse crowd,
Surging back to city streets for ale and chops and tarts.
And in the winter evening Tiger Bay *was* Tiger Bay,
And the moon rose over the Severn Sea.

XXXIV

When we walked to Merthyr Tydfil, in the moonlight long ago,
When the mountain tracks were frozen and the crests were
    capped with snow,
We had tales and songs between us, and souls too young to fret,
And we had hopes and visions which the heart remembers yet.

The winds from the farthest mountains blew about us as we
    strode,
But we were warm and merry on the crooked freezing road,

And there were lamp-lit homesteads to south and east and west
And we watched the round moon smiling on those little lights
of rest.

The moon is still as radiant and the homely hills remain,
But the magic of those evenings we shall not meet again,
For we were boyish dreamers in a world we did not know
When we walked to Merthyr Tydfil in the moonlight long ago.

XXXV

The night winds shake the tall trees above the hillside graves ;
Awake them not, O night winds, awake them not to-night ;
Let them not know our crazier, sorrier plight ;
O night winds, do not murmur to our fathers in their graves.
But blow about us, night wind and dawn wind and wild wind,
Until one greater man shall lead us
And our hearts be young again.

Perhaps the enduring mountains shall stir our blood again,
That earth shall sing of glory before the best have died,
That all things mean and squalid shall pass for ever away,
But though our hope be fragile let us keep faith with pride !
And on a peak in Gwalia, I babble in the night :
The cargoes steam from Cardiff, and Cardiff streets are bright,
The trains flash down the valleys, the land is fresh with light,
The horny hands have honour, and Love alone has might.

For *Selected Poems* (1953) Idris Davies changed line 6 of this poem to :
Until one greater day shall greet us

XXXVI

In the places of my boyhood
  The pit-wheels turn no more,
Nor any furnace lightens
  The midnight as of yore.

The slopes of slag and cinder
  Are sulking in the rain,
And in derelict valleys
  The hope of youth is slain.

And yet I love to wander
  The early ways I went,
And watch from doors and bridges
  The hills and skies of Gwent.

Though blighted be the valleys
  Where man meets man with pain,
The things my boyhood cherished
  Stand firm, and shall remain.

[Gwalia Deserta

HYWEL AND BLODWEN

Where are you going to, Hywel and Blodwen,
With your eyes as sad as your shoes ? NO money ?
We are going to learn a nimble language Unemployed
By the waters of the Ouse.

We are tramping through Gloucester and through Leicester,
We hope we shall not drop,
And we talk as we go of the Merthyr streets
And a house at Dowlais Top.

We have triads and englyns from pagan Dyfed
To brace us in the fight,
And three or four hundred Methodist hymns
To sing on a starless night.

We shall grumble and laugh and trudge together
Till we reach the stark North Sea
And talk till we die of Pantycelyn
And the eighteenth century.

We shall try to forget the Sunday squabbles,
And the foreign magistrate,
And the stupid head of the preacher's wife,
And the broken iron gate.

So here we say farewell and wish you
Less trouble and less pain,
And we trust you to breed a happier people
Ere our blood flows back again.

· movement of communities **49**
- emigration
- Govt policies

DIWEDD AWST

Mae'r haf yn cilio, cilio,
A 'madael rhaid i mi,
O diroedd teg Frycheiniog
P'le gân fy nghalon i.

A bydd fy nghalon yno
Fel 'deryn yn y ddôl,
A minnau heb un galon
Ymhlith y miloedd ffôl.

O bydd ger Afon Llundain
Rhyw grwydryn ffôl, digwsg,
Yn sibrwd am ei galon
A ganai ger yr Wysg.

1936

(At the end of August a nostalgic Silurian teacher-poet, conscious of the need soon to leave inspiring Brecknock hills for a more heartless urban existence, contrasts the Thames and Usk rivers as sources of song.)

THE ROSES OF THE SKY

It may be that when I am old and grey
    and sad and wise
I shall not see those vast roses brightening
    in the summer skies,
But now that I am young and foolish
    with a head full of dreams
I see the great roses of heaven reflected
    in all lakes and streams.

I see their brilliant petals opening and
    trembling and softly fading to gold,
And I know their hearts are secure and
    happy and will never be old,
And when those great petals are still, the lands
    are beautiful and the seas and the skies,
And I must gaze dearly upon them, before I
    grow grey and wise.

Summer, 1935

WILLIAM BUTLER YEATS

In his youth he ran through the tempests
To the edge of the sorrowful wave
And he gathered the beauty of sorrow,
And was noble in all that he gave.

In the autumn of life he vanquished
The paltry, the base, and the blind,
And the foes that he scattered before him
Saw a terrible radiance behind.

31st December, 1936

A DREAM IN SLIGO

One night I dreamed in Sligo
  That Yeats again was young,
A boy upon Ben Bulben
  With melody on his tongue.

He wandered alone and listened
  To the reeds of Knocknarea,
And with his dreams to the Rosses
  He came at close of day.

And suddenly he gathered
  Out of the lonely sea
A rod to strike the lonelier waves
  Of human memory.

A RAGGED MERCHANT

In that crazy and beautiful country
   God made when the moon was bright,
I tramped with a dead man's fiddle
   And played it by day and by night
To the old and the young and the reckless
   In the counties of Galway and Clare,
And I was drunk with the dancing
   And the tang of the sea in the air.

O I was a ragged merchant
   With all the old tunes to sell,
And I cared not a hang for the favours
   Or the frowns of Heaven or Hell,
And I dozed at the side of my fiddle
   When the moon rose out of the sea,
And I dreamed of the other old fiddlers
   Who were ten times as merry as me.

IRISH RAILWAY STATION

The village road is drying in the wind,
And whitening, narrowing to the distant hill ;
The clouds are tumbling slowly from the west
And lanky Michael dangles four dead hares
And shuffles and curses by the gate.
The steeple and the chimneys ignore the window lights,
A rising wind torments the telegraph wires.
And I stare through the carriage window
As the grey dusk slowly dies ;
Half listening to the wind ; half listening to the voices
Of Ireland from doorstep, hedgerow, farmstead, village store.
And I see blocks of turf against a stormy sky,
And dark-shawled women in threes and fours,
And an old man shaking his fist at the moon,
And Oliver Goldsmith swaggering in green,
Scattering fairies with a walking-stick,
And somewhere in the darkness Robert Emmet hoists a
    torch,
And the graves of Glasnevin are white in the sun,
And Cuchulain is shouting from a cairn . . .
But jolt, jolt, jolt, and engine whistle, and again we rattle on
To the starlit harbour of Rosslare.

1938

THE COAST OF KERRY

And suddenly in this 'bus at Moorgate
I recall the coast of Kerry in the evening drizzle,
The mists low and dark along the nearest islands,
A square brown cottage, the long garden, and wet pink roses,
And Mrs. Farrell bidding a brisk goodnight
To the smooth new priest
Whose eyes are on the snarling spaniel ;
Then we talk for an hour by the kitchen fire,
Talk of Dublin and sugar-beet and dialect,
And of the youth I met one day
Upon the bridge in Sligo,
The youth who had never heard of Yeats or Innisfree !
Then in comes Martin Murphy from the rain,
Mr. Murphy the tourist from Birmingham,
With his sentimental praise of the Irish weather . . .
The lamp is lit, and I listen to the far sea-murmur,
And I think of the mists along the broken coast,
The cry of the sea-fowl, and I wonder
If the sea-fowl are really sorrowful,
And I remember the beautiful prose of Synge
And somehow believe he is not dead.

EIRE

I remember crimson mountains
  Far away and fading blue,
And the shyness of the shamrock,
  And the barn cocks greeting Lugh.

And the white walls, and the donkeys
  Slowly treading to the shore,
And the gipsies down in Kerry,
  And the fiddler of Tramore.

And a woman wandering wildly
  With her sorrow in her mirth,
And the dream that is Glasnevin
  Where the dead defy the earth.

And I know I shall remember
  Till the heart within me dies,
Bells of Galway, falling, fading,
  In the distant skies.

Easter, 1944

DUBLIN

Where Jonathan Swift is a heap of dust,
   And Joyce is a bell in the air,
Where Yeats once walked in a coat of dreams,
   In joy and in despair,
I walk tonight and brood in the rain
   That blows to the Irish Sea,
I brood like a fool in a bout of farce
   That follows the tragedy.

And the Liffey sings as she sang for Joyce,
   As she sings for the lout and the sage,
And the desolate quays await the ghosts
   Out of a turbulent age,
Out of a past that was reckless with pride
   And wild with sacrifice—
And lo, as I pass, the spectres grin
   On the flesh that paid the price.

GLASNEVIN

High summer on Glasnevin
And Dublin in a haze,
And who among these sacred mounds
Forgets the bitter days ?

Here Parnell rests for ever
From love and agony,
And all those saints and sinners
Who stormed eternity.

Here lanky Michael Collins
Is young for evermore,
And the Countess hears for ever
Drums on the Danaan shore.

The young, the wild, the eloquent
Are silent, and at rest,
And the lilies shine and tremble
In a wind from the west.

IN GLASNEVIN CEMETERY

In this garden of great memories, this latter Clonmacnoise,
Where the great tumult has died down
And where two Easters are remembered for ever—
The first strange Easter of the Syrian hills
And that other that shone on the Dublin quays—
I stand and remember the pride of Padraig Pearse
And the pride of Connolly ; and I seek the quiet glade
Where the ravaged heart of Parnell
Sleeps beneath a rugged Wicklow stone ;
And I gaze on the sealed coffin of Daniel O'Connell
That lies so perfect in its silence, and so superbly careless
Of all the days, the hours, of earth and flesh and time.
Here where a people's pride is renewed and nourished
For ever beneath the vast and naked heavens,
Here I muse and ponder on the price that pride must pay,
Here I turn and suddenly see across the summer sky
The black tips and the little square chapels of Wales,
And I hear the sentimental sighs of a people watching
Its ancient hills and pastures filched acre by acre
By the vulgar claws of a blind bureaucracy.
I only hear the sentimental songs of a people
Most careless of their heritage, and here and there
A little piper playing his pacifistic tune,
The mockery of peace. Owain Glyndwr piped not thus,
But Owain Glyndwr's dead, and the land he died to save
Forgets the cry he raised against the filching earls.
The land he loved has grown a Calvinistic beard
To guard its nonconformist conscience,
The land he loved is full of little squalid chapels
Where the solemn sit down to squabble and sigh . . .

But Pearse and Macdonagh, and the Countess of the drums,
The dreamers and the fighters who fought to save their dreams,
They strode out from their shadowy echoing churches,
They strode out and fought and died
And they redeemed their land from many shames
And left the name of Dublin splendid among cities,
And made this white Glasnevin a garden of glory.

1951

GOLD

Whatever the future brings us, the past has brought us gold,
For this land was a land of singing in the stirring days of old,
When Spenser roamed through dreamland and Marlowe was afire,
But Shakespeare out of Arden, his was the sweetest lyre.

Then England bred a Milton whose voice shall never die,
A Virgil born in London who flared beyond the sky,
And a Blake sat down with angels to wrangle and rejoice,
But Shakespeare out of Arden, his was the golden voice.

And a Coleridge, fed on manna, was mighty in his day,
And a Shelley, swift and radiant, went dazzling on his way,
And a Yeats arose in splendour to sing of a nation's wrong,
But Shakespeare out of Arden, his was the perfect song.

WILLIAM MORRIS

Because the mind is growing cold,
A slave that bends to the God of Gold,
We have no time to learn your lay,
Sweet singer of an idle day.

We have great problems and great pains
And gas-mask drills and aeroplanes ;
We would not understand your way,
Sweet singer of an idle day.

We have no frenzy in the heart,
We play a mean mechanic part—
You would not understand our way,
Sweet singer of an idle day.

We honour dolts in racing cars
And dirty dogs and talkie stars ;
Our fields are brown, our children grey,
O singer of an idle day !

Highgate, 1937

NEMESIS

The hierarchies of angels
    Have vanished from the sky,
And folk aver that Heaven
    Was but a cunning lie,
And curates out of college,
    Like the poets of the plains,
Stand up for all things modern—
    But Nemesis remains.

Apollo and Athena,
    They dwell no more in Greece—
Though the glory that was Athens
    Is a song that shall not cease—
And Pan and all his pipers,
    And Bacchus and his trains
Have left the summer islands—
    But Nemesis remains.

The gods of Scandinavia
    Have perished in the snow,
And Arthur and his Merlin
    Have gone as shadows go,
And we talk of foods synthetic
    And scientific brains
And the debt we owe to Darwin—
    But Nemesis remains.

Our morals are as roses
　　That fade ere summer dies,
And Hollywood is Zion
　　To ten million modern eyes,
And from our concrete towers
　　We hurl the hoary chains
That bound us to the temples—
　　But Nemesis remains.

CUCKOO

Cry, cuckoo, over the listless corn
  And the unkilled meat,
And Morgan's bony pony
  Nosing in the street.

Cry, cuckoo, over rivers
  Brown and slow and dumb,
Pity the rural virgin,
  Also the crowded slum.

Cry, cuckoo, to the spire
  Over the market town,
Worry the auctioneer
  Born in the County Down.

Cry, cuckoo, to the hiker,
  The student of escape,
Answer the toddler's echo,
  Give it a classic shape.

Cry, cuckoo, to the tavern
  Where duffers dote on darts,
And mock the pretty poet
  Who lives by fits and starts.

Cry, cuckoo, to the mayor
   Planting the penny tree
And to the sad black women
   Who visit the cemetery.

Cry once more to this valley,
   Cuckold the heart and brain,
Before you depart from Gwalia
   For somewhere south of Spain.

CONTRACEPTION

Sing a song of contraception
   Now that spring is come again,
Shun the fruit of copulation
   And run no risk of pain.

Ours is such a civilisation
   That the seed of man is best
Destroyed, so that our population
   Shall not put us to the test.

See the lords of all creation
   Afraid to multiply their kind !
See how nation watches nation
   While the figures fall behind !

See distorted education
   Serve a system based on lies,
See a nervous generation
   Pretending to be wise.

Yet behold the conflagration,
   Harvests burning in the night,
Destruction out of desperation
   To keep the profits right.

Shun the fruit of copulation
   Lest a famine come your way,
Sing a song of contraception
   And let the harvests burn away.

April, 1938

EZE-SUR-MER

The jewelled sea,
the orange east,
the purpled road
to the fabled beast.

Naked and smooth
beyond the vine,
O singer from Cyprus
make every word shine !

From the bitter land
I came to this shore,
to the peacock, the fig,
the pirate's lore.

Drab were the nations
trading in gold ;
O sun and O grape,
give joy as of old !

EL GRECO

His light leaps round the brain,
His shadows encroach on the heart,
And I remember a broken tower
Against the setting sun,
And sounds of battle in the heavens,
Tempestuous trumpets through the night
Over a thousand years ago ;
And I saw the bloodstained city,
Beggars in purple angry on the mountains
And the vast beard of God afire.

SECURITY

I have seen again the man of dusk,
The lonely man who does not bend to words.
I have touched his long white hands
And seen his body in unwilling grass.
Between the water and the stone he cries
Of great wings whirling in the east
And silver ghosts that scorn a tawdry world.
Who shall reveal the root of life
And who shall tell where all light fades ?
It is safer to be sane among the crowds
In the familiar places, safer to be dumb,
To keep within the flesh the mystery,
To lock within the heart the word.

INTERLUDE

And now that man prepares for doom
I bring a bullfinch on my thumb
And I walk and walk around Trafalgar Square
And up the Strand to the dusty bed of Donne
Where my bullfinch pipes in the shadow of frozen
    laughter,
Pipes on of health and mirth and corn and wine
In the valleys that unmated birds imagine
When flocks awake to cross the April sea.
O happy boy on my London thumb,
Sing for an hour when sunset drapes
The riverside with strange embroidery,
And pipe your loudest when the placards scream
Of disasters and dictators, and drugs to save the world.

1938

THE CANARY

The yellow bird sings behind the bars
    At three in the afternoon,
The yellow bird sings as he sang last year—
O can there be time to him more dear ?—
    At three in the afternoon.

The yellow bird sings as though he were born
    For three in the afternoon,
The yellow bird sings and no one heeds,
And he whistles though all the village bleeds,
    At three in the afternoon.

The yellow bird sings for very joy
    At three in the afternoon—
O comes there a vision to him of far trees,
The palm and the orange, the orchids, the seas,
    At three in the afternoon ?

THE NEUTER FOLK

We are the bloodless hybrids of the dusk,
We do not murder or caress,
We look at stones, and pass ;
We know not fame nor infamy ;
We doubt not, neither do we sing.

Few, few shall greet where many meet
At six o'clock in Liverpool Street.

Our armies are trenched in No Man's Land,
Our loaded rifles are in wool,
Our scouts find no enemy.
There is no foe nor friend to know
Our lack of plan and strategy.
Our prophets know nor joy nor sorrow,
Our wantons do not fall.
Our larders are of dead dreams full,
And after dinner we are bland,
And ask, 'Which way shall we go ?'

THE SACRIFICE

And a young man rose from the grave
On a cool cloudless morning,
And his flesh was grey and blistered,
And he lifted yellow eyes
Toward the rising sun.
Stretching his body, he groaned,
And gazed at the crimson glow in the east ;
And because the sky was beautiful,
And mountain-tops in the distance sparkled with life
(A mule brayed then among the reeds and stones),
And because he imagined children in far-off valleys laughing,
He said : ' This body will stain the luminous earth '.
And he smiled wanly, then closed his eyes,
And crept back into the grave.

1938

THE GATE OF DEATH

I remember a little of the gate of death ;
There was not any light, nor leaf, nor sound,
Only a great silence among stones.
And I shuddered and tried to call to the world,
But my tongue was as dumb as the rock ;
And I could not remember the faces of parents or friends,
I could only wait and tremble.
Only of loneliness was I aware.
And suddenly came a voice from the vast and hollow night.
' I will call you in some other hour. You will come '.
And then I felt my hands and my brow and my limbs,
And I ran to a place of sunlight and heather
And I pressed my body to the warm brown soil,
And wept, and bit the grass for joy.

1939

ONE FEBRUARY EVENING

Now in these mountain grasses beneath a winter sky
I watch the valleys lighted, I hear the curlew cry,
I hear the sorrowful echoes borne from the Severn Sea,
And the dirge of desolation, the sigh of history.

O mountain grasses ignorant of man and all his pain,
Sing in this freezing twilight, murmur to me again
Of the prehistoric aeons, the landscapes pure and bare,
The centuries of silence, the unpolluted air.

O northern winds, my lovers, roar around me where I stand,
A naked creature lonely in a brown and barren land,
And scatter from my memory the weeds of human lore
And make me as cold, as careless, as a wave on a desolate
    shore.

1939

DUNKIRK 1940

(For Z. and B.)

The little ships, the little ships
  Rushed out across the sea
To save the luckless armies
  From death and slavery.

From Tyne and Thames and Tamar,
  From the Severn and the Clyde,
The little ships, the little ships
  Went out in all their pride.

And home they brought their warriors,
  Weary and ragged and worn,
Back to the hills and shires
  And the towns where they were born.

Three hundred thousand warriors,
  From Hell to Home they came,
In the little ships, the little ships
  Of everlasting fame.

They were the sons of the common people
   And they were the kings of the air,
Their triumph shall be told for ever,
   Their fame be always fair.

They rose to save the land of Britain,
   They scattered the foe to the sea,
And blazoned across the roaring heavens
   The arcs of victory.

O they were young and swift and valiant,
   Braced to battle and to dare,
And they were the sons of the common people
   And they were the kings of the air.

CRADLE SONG

The searchlights are playing all over the sky,
And the young men of Europe are sailing on high
Dealing death and destruction to the homes on the plain
And leaving behind them grief, anger and pain.

And out of the darkness flashes shell after shell
And earth is the playground of the powers of Hell,
And mother's wee baby is sleeping so sound,
O mother's wee baby is sleeping so sound !

February, 1941, Anstey, Hertfordshire

POEM

A child shall seek compassion
And find the world is dead ;
Flame and ruin and charred flesh.
Yesterday we drank beneath the cherry tree
And pondered on folk who fall
Prey to scientific monsters.
The slaughter then was in another town
Beyond the friendly mountain,
And it was almost sweet to express the sorrow.
But now the last child wanders alone,
And love, and even language,
Are not found any more,
And two little feet shall run in desperation,
Until the nightmare is part of eternity.

AIR RAID

So here we are at last in the trenches
Facing the dusty war memorial,
And the evening wind surges from the west ;
With gas-masks dangling from our fists,
With our eyes and ears as those of the hunted fox,
And our feet in the grooved clay,
Crouching and huddling together,
Trusting, and faintly believing that death will pass us by,
Our minds too frightened to reflect
Upon the war memorial.
(Yesterday we chuckled at the irony,
Today irony is a luxury known only to minds at peace.)
And what is the use of lamenting
That the sacrifice of millions was in vain,
What is the use of lamenting now ?
Their world is destroyed for ever,
And our world is a valley of guns and shadows.
Too late now to lament, to weep, to pray.
Too late now to recall virtue and respectability,
And all the suffering we never deserved,
Too late now to sigh beneath the everlasting cypress tree.
The dying have learnt that death is not romantic,
The living shall learn what the dying must forget.
So pardon us you boys who marched away
To lie and sigh and die in the mud of foreign fields,
Pardon us that we remember no heroes tonight,
That we only think of the bombers above us, and the clay below
    us, and the blood within us.

Pardon us tonight as we crouch in these trenches
Unashamed of our fears,
We who have dreamed of peace on earth,
And allowed the gun to dominate the world.

So you old folk and you toddlers and you weary mothers,
Crouch down, keep still, weep not,
Weep not, for life and death will regard not your weeping,
Crouch down, and be still, be still.
From the far moist west the night wind blows
And the echoes of your sorrow will only be echoes
Dying on the careless winds—
Look, they come, they come !
See, the lights are nearer, nearer, nearer,
A swift tumultuous bracelet of lights !
Crouch down for the sake of the flesh upon your bones,
Crouch nearer the clay, O man made in the image of God !
Crouch down and pretend to be cool and brave,
Crouch down, and babble to your inmost self
Of home and love and luck, and life, O life ! O life !

MEESDEN IN HERTFORDSHIRE

The autumn came so proudly here,
But the winter was so drear
 With dead brown trees
 And shivering knees,
And a funeral full of fear.

Over the frozen fields of dawn
The melancholy brain would spawn
 Creatures unknown to human life
 And wholly given to sickly strife
Whence the mares of night were drawn.

And when the moon arose behind
The legendary hart and hind
 A farmer crouched behind the reeds,
 Remembering all the unchronicled deeds
In the shadows of the caverns of the mind.

THE ANGRY SUMMER

A poem of 1926

I

Now it is May among the mountains,
Days for speeches in the valley towns,
Days of dream and days of struggle,
Days of bitter denunciation.

Now it is May in all the valleys,
Days of the cuckoo and the hawthorn,
Days for splashing in the mountain ponds,
Days for love in crowded parks.

Now it is May in little gardens,
In square allotments across the railway,
Days for song and dance and roaming,
Days for action and achievement.

Now it is May in the minds of men,
Days for vision and for marching,
Days for banners and for music,
And beauty born of sacrifice.

[The Angry Summer

2

From Abertillery and Aberdare
  And Rhondda Fach and Rhondda Fawr
And Ogmore Vale and Nine Mile Point
  And Bargoed and Brynmawr,
The delegates come in morning trains
  To meet in Cardiff City,
And some have tongues and some have brains
  And some pretend they're witty,
And some have come with hearts aflame
  To plead and plan and fight
For those who toil without a name
  And pass into the night.

3

Now is the month of Maying
When collier lads are playing,
And many mothers sighing,
Tra la la la la la,
And miners' leaders threatening,
And royalty owners cursing,
And Dan the Grocer vexing,
Tra la la la la la,
Now is the month of marching,
Valley to valley calling,
Bugle to bugle replying,
Tra la la la la la,
Brother to brother responding,
Woman to woman complaining,
Mountain to mountain shining,
Banner to banner waving,
Tra la la la la la.

4

Tonight the moon is bright and round
Above the little burial ground
Where father of Dai and father of John
After the sweat and blood sleep on.

They do not hear your voice tonight,
O singer on the slaggy height,
They do not know the song you sing
Of battle on this night of spring.

Repeat-
old
challenge
But in their blood in Maytimes past
The armies of the future massed,
And in their dreams your dreams were born,
Out of their night shall break your morn.

Chronicler
Shine softly, moon, upon their sleep,
And, poet, in your music keep
Their memory alive and fair,
Echoing through the electric air.

The Strike

What will you do with your shovel, Dai,
And your pick and your sledge and your spike,
And what will you do with your leisure, man,
Now that you're out on strike ?

Financial
What will you do for your butter, Dai,
And your bread and your cheese and your fags,
And how will you pay for a dress for the wife,
aspects And shall your children go in rags ?

[*The Angry Summer*

You have been, in your time, a hero, Dai, *Public*
And they wrote of your pluck in the press, *attitudes*
And now you have fallen on evil days,
And who will be there to bless ?

And how will you stand with your honesty, Dai,
When the land is full of lies, — *slander*
And how will your curb your anger, man,
When your natural patience dies ?

O what will you dream on the mountains, Dai,
When you walk in the summer day,
And gaze on the derelict valleys below,
And the mountains farther away ?

And how will the heart within you, Dai,
Respond to the distant sea,
And the dream that is born in the blaze of the sun,
And the vision of victory ?

6

Stand up, and tell the robbers *Revenge.*
'Tis time to drop the swag,
Avenge our cheated fathers, *gladstone.*
Who bled for Viscount Bag.

Owners

'Tis time to scale the ramparts
That guard the bloody swag,
And speak appropriate language
To dropsical Viscount Bag.

Mrs. Evans fach, you want butter again.
How will you pay for it now, little woman
With your husband out on strike, and full
Of the fiery language ? Ay, I know him,
His head is full of fire and brimstone
And a lot of palaver about communism,
And me, little Dan the Grocer
Depending so much on private enterprise.

What, depending on the miners and their
Money too ? O yes, in a way, Mrs. Evans,
Yes, in a way I do, mind you.
Come tomorrow, little woman, and I'll tell you then
What I have decided overnight.
Go home now and tell that rash red husband of yours
That your grocer cannot afford to go on strike
Or what would happen to the butter from Carmarthen?
Good day for now, Mrs. Evans fach.

8

O that my passion would fuse
The valleys I love to flame,
The valleys of decent homes
Threatened by shadows of shame.

O valleys that gave me birth,
And comradeship and song,
Before I go back to the earth
May my eyes see the end of this wrong.

[*The Angry Summer*

From these broken hills of my home,
Haunts of my boyhood and youth,
I want to shout of the shadows that pass
In the sunshine and splendour of truth.

The Press ?

9

So you have come down from London ;
    O young man in plus fours,
To write about our troubles
    In slick and popular prose ?

Say, are you a slave from London   *partizan*
    Who write what you are told
By a brazen man of millions   *Press*
    Whose only creed is gold ?

Or have you come for knowledge,   *biased*
    Solid and plain and bare,
And have you a love for honesty
    To teach you how to dare ?

Do you value the code of comrades
    And the decency of life,
And the pride that spurns the traitor
    In the roaring hour of strife ?

But if you come here to slander
    And trade in yellow lies,   *pro-conservative*
Go back, young man, to London,
    With shame between your eyes.

The Angry Summer]

10

High summer on the mountains
And on the clover leas,
And on the local sidings,
And on the rhubarb leaves.

Brass bands in all the valleys
Blaring defiant tunes,
Crowds, acclaiming carnival,
Prize pigs and wooden spoons.

Still on strike

Dust on shabby hedgerows
Behind the colliery wall,
Dust on rail and girder
And tram and prop and all.

High summer on the slag heaps
And on polluted streams,
And old men in the morning
Telling the town their dreams.

11

Press, law and authority are against the miners

See the pompous magistrate
Heavy in wit and heavy in gait,
A pudding on a wooden plate.

See the men go one by one
Tanned by mountain breeze and sun
Defending every action done.

See the sun go down in flame
Above the tower that cannot tame
The pearls that challenged days of shame.

[*The Angry Summer*

CHURCH IN MIDDLE [handwritten]

12

'Tis very embarrassing, say what you like,
To be a good vicar in a valley on strike
And preach Christian fellowship on Sunday night
To men and women who are forced to fight
For bread and cheese. How shall I handle this text from St. Paul ?
(There's that meeting outside the vicarage wall.
O dear, O dear, these politics ! Drat them, I say !
I would I were living much further away.)
And some of those leaders quote scripture with ease
As though they had spent all their nights on their knees.
(That's Margaret upstairs singing love songs again !)
I must make up my mind, make the issue plain,
I must be honest with honest men,
Bless them in battle, and speak on their side,
And gather my courage, and envy their pride !

13

Loves his home [handwritten]

O the lands of Usk are dear
    And all the woods of Wye,
And the magic shores of Dyfed
    Beneath the summer sky.

But the blackened slopes of Rhymney
    I saw with childhood's eye,
These shall be dearer, dearer,
    When I must turn to die.

14

I could point out a rascal here and there
And damn the lot because of a few—
Sometimes a cloud will darken the town
But far beyond the hills are blue.

I could say of John and Will and Ned
They waste too much on cards and beer,
And perhaps they could be blamed as much
For lecherous days as the sons of a peer.

I could say that Marged Jane has lazy hours
Spent in gossiping over the broom,
And mark out a daughter here and there
Who craves the flesh though the end be doom.

I could preach you a sermon on the sin
Of putting the belly before the soul—
And so damn the ladies in satin and silk
Who play with the lords in the Metropole.

I could say much more of the men I know
And damn myself with hypocrisy—
I would rather salute the men who dare
To strike at the roots of their misery.

15

In the square brown chapel below the hill
Dai's frail mother is deep in prayer,
A broken old mother who bears no ill
To anyone anywhere.

[*The Angry Summer*

' Please God have blessings for us all
And comfort them who mourn,
And have mercy on me in my humble shawl,
And melt the hearts of stone.'

The sun's last light is passing away,
And a moth flits to and fro,
And out in the street the children play
And the echoes softly go.

' O Brother who came from Nazareth
To help and heal and save,
O Lord of life and Lord of death,
Help my old heart to be brave.'

16

Great are the fires of Ebbw Vale,
And all the seas and the heavens,
Great are the ships in Barry Dock
And great the golden forests,
Great are the shadows over the Rhondda
And the mansions built in the shires,
Great are the fortunes made in Gwalia
And the promontories of slag.

'Tis time to go to America
And tell an impressive tale,
Or money will flow across the sea
And this strike will never fail.

'Tis time we told in Washington
Of men who will not see
The necessity for settlement
And the profits for you and me.

'Tis time to go to Wall Street
And beat the strikers down—
Though we do it behind their backs—
To save the banks of London Town.

Man alive, what a belly you've got !
You'll take all the serge in my little shop.
Stand still for a minute, now, and I'll get your waist.
Man alive, what a belly you've got !
Oh, I know it's only a striker's pay you get,
But don't misunderstand me, Hywel bach ;
I depend for my bread on working men
And I am only a working man myself
Just Shinkin Rees the little tailor,
Proud of my work and the people I serve ;
And I wouldn't deny you a suit for all the gold in all the world.
Just pay me a little each week, Hywel bach,
And I am your tailor as long as you live,
Shinkin Rees your friend and your tailor,
Proud to serve you, and your dear old father before you.
But man alive, what a belly you've got !

[*The Angry Summer*

' These are your children begging for bread,
You foolish miners ! ' the newspaper said.
' Look at the pictures that all may see—
Victims of your stupidity !
O you stubborn, callous men,
Starving your kids and wives again,
Striking because the weather is fair,
And leaving your collieries out of repair,
And drinking your beer as if you had right
To share in the joys of a summer night.
Once you were heroes, you rescued your kind
Out of the galleries left blazing behind,
And we praised you in eloquent journalese
And chattered about you at parlour teas.
And now you won't work for your daily bread
You lazy miners ! ' the newspaper said.

20

Look at the valleys down there in the darkness,
Long bracelets of twinkling lights,
And here with the mountain breeze on your brow
Consider the folk in the numberless streets
Between the long dark ridges, north to south.
Township after township lit up in long broken lines,
Silent and sparkling, sprinkling with jewels the night,
And Mrs. Hughes and Mrs. Rees rushing from shop to shop,
All fuss and bother, and Gwyneth and Blodwen
And slim young men hurrying now to the sixpenny dance,
And Shoni Bach Morris away to his pint,

The Angry Summer]

95

And Ned and his wife and his kids in a crowd
Intent on the glamour of Hollywood ;
Street intersecting street, and memorial clock in the circle,
The chemist's window radiant with cures for all complaints,
Lovers holding hands outside the furniture stores,
Bright buses sliding in from east and west,
And here's the toothless, barefoot old sailor at the corner
Yelling a song for your little brown penny.
London in little for one night in the week,
Red lights and green lights, and crowded pavements,
And who cares a damn on one night at least,
One night of tinsel, one night of jazz.
And one by one the lights shall go out
In all the valleys, leaving isolated lamps, silver pins,
Sticking into the inverted velvet of the midnight air.
And you shall listen then to the silence
That is not silence, to the murmur
Of the uneasy centuries among the ancient hills and valleys
As here you stand with the mountain breeze on your brow.

Glad to be on strike.

21

Let us tramp to the summer shires
And play on violins
Among the clover meadows
And the apple blossom there.
The skies are vast and cloudless
And all the flowers of June
Shall sway and sparkle around us
As we play on violins.

[*The Angry Summer*

And perhaps the farmers and their folk
Will be our friends and greet us
And know the truth behind the battle
As we play on violins.
We shall sleep among the haystacks
And the hedgerows and the barns,
And wake to the morning songs
Of all the birds in Breconshire,
Music wilder and sweeter
Than we play on violins.
O let us be off to the countryside
And tramp by the Usk and the Wye,
And sing of the summer battle
As we play on violins.

22

Shoni bach Amos drunk again !
And your whiskers long and white,
And your nose as red as a sunset
And your old, old eyes so bright.

Shoni bach Amos drunk again !
And merry as twenty three,
Singing of cronies and wenches
And the fun that used to be.

Shoni bach Amos drunk again !
Drunk as a lord in town,
Forgetting the life-long squalor
That kept you and your children down.

23

O young man alone in the Workmen's Reading Room
Poring for hours over words and words,
Delighting in the magic phrase, stirred by the eloquent line,
Will you sit and forget the facts of the hour,
And indulge in the butterfly trivialities
Produced by spinsters in pleasant gardens
In inland spas and resorts by the sea ?
Or will you remain alert and determined
And cull from your reading the blossoms of truth,
Bring generous impulses to gather and treasure
All honest and beautiful thoughts and deeds ?
O young man so ardent, rich in your dreams,
Make precious each hour, and grasp while you may,
And give ear, O give ear in the cool of the dusk,
To the magnificent orchestras of history.

Cow-parsley and hawthorn blossom
And a cottage among trees,
A thrush and a skylark singing,
And a gipsy lying at ease.

Roses in gentlemen's gardens
Smile as we pass by the way,
And the swans of my lord are sleeping
Out of the heat of the day.

And here we come tramping and singing
Out of the valleys of strife,
Into the sunlit cornlands,
Begging the bread of life.

[*The Angry Summer*

He won't talk any more of the distant days
Of his childhood in the coalface and the tavern
And all his cronies who had left him behind
In the ragged little hut by the river ;
He who had given so much of his sweat
In the days of his youth and his vigour,
Now falling like a wrinkled apple into a ditch
To rot away in the everlasting dust of death.
Tonight he shall sleep in a grave on the slope,
And no more will he prattle of the days of his youth.
Days of the Truck System and the Tory Sabbath,
And the Chartists and the starved-out strikers.
No more will he lean on the bridge in the summer **morning**
And make a god of Gladstone and a devil of Disraeli,
And go into raptures on the young Lloyd George
Who strode into London with a dazzling sword,
A bright St. David from the stormy mountain.
All his long and luckless days are over,
And the broken old body in the plain deal coffin
Will be deaf to all the birds above the hill,
The larks that sing and sing in the cloudless sky
As the men move away in slow black clusters
Down on the road to the colliery town.

26

Where did you get that big black cock
That wakes the street in the morning ?
Did he win you a prize in the County show,
And did he win it for crowing ?

Did you breed him, Dai, in your own backyard
And try to make him a tenor ?
And did he go on strike for yellower corn
And lose his voice in a temper ?

27

These men went into the gloom
And the danger day by day,
Went down with a curse and a joke
And believed that Britain should be
Greater for all their toil.
And then when the profits were high
And the bags of gold were full,
The men who created the gold
Were told that the time was come
To lower the standards of life
And exist on fewer loaves,
Less meat and butter and cheese.
So out of the grime they came,
Insulted and angry and proud,
Together to march in the sun
With a song and a curse and a vow,
Together to challenge the creed
That blood is baser than gold,
Together to stand to the end,
Together to live or die.

[*The Angry Summer*

28

Hywel and Olwen are alone in the fern
On the hills behind the town,
Talking and kissing with lips that burn
As the sun of June goes down.

' O how can we marry, Olwen, my love,
With me on a striker's pay ?
How will you manage a home, my love,
Through the troubles of the day ? '

' I will face all the troubles as others do,
Hywel my darling, my love,
And share in your battle through and through,
And live and die for love ! '

Hywel and Olwen lie warm in the fern
With passionate mouth on mouth
And the lights in the valley twinkle and turn
And the moon climbs up from the south.

In the Admiral Nelson the lads are together,
And Lizzie the barmaid is rippling with fun,
And on Saturday night the beer is good.

The darts whizz past the full flushed faces,
And the old men chuckle with yellow teeth,
And on Saturday night the beer is good.

The fiddler's mate crawls round with a cap,
' Our Tommy is going to college some day ',
And on Saturday night the beer is good.

The sawdust is bright for the first half hour,
' Lloyd George was the boy to talk to the Lords ',
And on Saturday night the beer is good.

The curate calls in for a box of matches,
' My old Martha was full of the devil today ',
And on Saturday night the beer is good.

30

They chased us out of the summer shires,
From the lands of the Usk and the Wye,
And cursed us in bitter language
And hoped we would starve and die.

They sent their hounds to tear us
And yokels with sporting guns,
As if we had been the Vandals,
The Zulus, and the Huns.

They chased us across the pastures,
Through woods, and over streams,
And called us knaves and rascals,
Lazy and crazy with dreams.

And back we trudged to the valleys,
Amused and tired and brown,
But our violins were playing
When we reached the mining town.

[*The Angry Summer*

Let's go to Barry Island, Maggie fach,
And give all the kids one day by the sea,
And sherbet and buns and paper hats,
And a rattling ride on the Figure Eight ;
We'll have tea on the sands, and rides on the donkeys,
And sit in the evening with the folk of Cwm Rhondda,
Singing the sweet old hymns of Pantycelyn
When the sun goes down beyond the rocky islands.
Come on, Maggie fach, or the train will be gone
Then the kids will be howling at home all day,
Sticky with dirt and gooseberry jam.
Leave the washing alone for today, Maggie fach,
And put on your best and come out to the sun
And down to the holiday sea.
We'll carry the sandwiches in a big brown bag
And leave our troubles behind for a day
With the chickens and the big black tips
And the rival soup-kitchens, quarrelling like hell.
Come, Maggie fach, with a rose on your breast
And an old Welsh tune on your little red lips,
And we'll all sing together in the Cardiff train
Down to the holiday sea.

Who loves not the land of his birth
Should hide himself in the earth.
Who loves not these derelict vales
Is no true son of eternal Wales.
Who curses not the vandal's crime
Is the simple pawn of lust and time.
Who learns no lesson from history
Sleeps in the slough of slavery.

Let us dance tonight in Tredegar,
Jazz to a lively tune,
Toss our troubles behind us,
Laugh with the girls of June.

Let us dance tonight for a tanner
And grab the warmest wench,
Have fish and chips for supper
And beer on the bench.

And across the moor at midnight
We'll walk back home again,
And arm in arm sing catches
From America and Spain.

[The Angry Summer

34

O summer night, O vast and fragrant night,
O night of flowers and mountain breezes,
O night that soothes the angry multitudes,
O velvet night that hides the valleys,
The humble homes among the broken hills,
That hides the dross until the dawn
And the bright warm day ; O night of June,
Give balm to worried minds and weary arms,
Caress with love the brows of little children
Who suffer subtly till the battle's done,
Refresh the honest heart that's ever bold
In thought and deed to beautify the world.
And give to man, O night of June, the power
Of proud and lovely speech to wake the world
From summer to summer, from year to year,
To wake the world to life, and life abundant,
And anthems worthy of triumphant days.

Community - struggle

35

' Would that we two were living
   In a cottage by the sea,
Away from these blackened valleys
   And the towns of misery.'

' No. Better the days of battle
   And the days of sacrifice
Among our own warm people
   Who have honest hands and eyes.'

' Would that we two were together
    Away from the bitter strife,
Safe from the demagogue's clamour
    And the fool's fanatic knife.'

' No. We shall stay among them,
    Giving the best of our lives
To the passionate men and women
    Who have honest hands and eyes.'

36

In the little Italian shop
Where they sell coloured gassy pop,
Listen to Emlyn tell his mate
How to organise the State,
How to end the troublous days
And lead the world to wiser ways.
Danny bach Dwl is eager, too,
To put an end to ballyhoo ;
And Nipper Evans would put things right
In this nation overnight.
One would make things brisk and hot,
Another kill the whole damn lot . . .
And on and on the chatter flows
Until Maria yawns and goes
To pull the blinds and shut the shop
So full of coloured gassy pop.

[The Angry Summer

37

Send out your homing pigeons, Dai,
Your blue-grey pigeons, hard as nails,
Send them with messages tied to their wings,
Words of your anger, words of your love.
Send them to Dover, to Glasgow, to Cork,
Send them to the wharves of Hull and of Belfast,
To the harbours of Liverpool and Dublin and Leith,
Send them to the islands and out of the oceans,
To the wild wet islands of the northern sea
Where little grey women go out in heavy shawls
At the hour of dusk to gaze on the merciless waters,
And send them to the decorated islands of the south
Where the mineowner and his tall stiff lady
Walk round and round the rose-pink hotel, day after day after
    day.
Send out your pigeons, Dai, send them out
With words of your anger and your love and your pride,
With stern little sentences wrought in your heart,
Send out your pigeons, flashing and dazzling towards the sun.

Go out, pigeons bach, and do what Dai tells you.

38

From Ammanford to Fleur-de-Lys
No honest man will bend the knee
To any parasitic band
Which battens on the ravaged land.

From Dowlais Top to Swansea Bay
The men are in the sun today
With angry hearts and fists of fire
To meet the challenge of the squire.

From Blaina down to Barry Dock
Dai and Glyn have set the clock
That points unto the judgement hour
For the vandal in his tower.

39

Put your arms around my body
And feed upon my breast,
And let your sorrow fade away
Into the darkening west.

In this hollow of the moorland
Young man, lie down with me,
And lose the day and its squalor
In the swoon of ecstasy.

Forget for tonight the tumult
The malice and the fret,
And know of the balm of my body
And clasp me and forget.

The hills and the vales are silent
And silent the stars above,
And my bosom is warm and gentle,
Young man, lie down and love.

[*The Angry Summer*

Only a penny, boys bach,
And a concert first-class,
So roll up now with your pennies
And help towards tomorrow's soup.
Our soprano is lovely to look at
With roses and lilies upon her,
And her voice is the sweetest in Wales ;
And our tenor will sing till you rise on your toes,
He will sing of the palms and the islands,
Of damsels, delightful, delicious,
And his eyes will be twinkling with mischief—
A tenor first-class, boys bach.
All the lads of the village will whistle
And the girls will be full of game,
And out of the heat of the broad afternoon
You will all sit together and listen
To a concert first-class for a penny
A little brown penny from under the china cow
On the end of the mantelpiece.
So come, boys bach, to a concert first-class
And help towards tomorrow's soup.

Here is Arthur J. Cook, a red rose in his lapel,
Astride on a wall, arousing his people,
Now with fist in the air, now a slap to the knee,
Almost burning his way to victory !

And tomorrow in all the hostile papers
There will be sneers at Cook and all his capers,
And cowardly scribblers will be busy tonight
Besmirching a warrior with the mud of their spite.

42

Among brown hills and black hills
   And hills bleak and bare
They have given us hovels
   And a bed and a chair
And told us to labour
   And not to desire
The cake of the countess,
   The wine of the squire.

But here we come marching
   And ready to dare
The wrath of the gamblers
   Who have dirtied the air,
And here we come singing
   The songs of our ire,
And with torches of beauty
   To set cities on fire.

43

O rain of July pouring down from the heavens,
Pouring and pelting from the vaults of the sky,
Pelting and slashing and lashing the trees,
Lashing the gardens behind the streets,
Sweeping the dust from the cabbage leaves,
And bringing Mrs. Hughes' pet geranium out to the garden wall,
Sweep away, thunder-rain, the dross from our valleys,
Carry the rubbish to the seas and the oceans,
Wash away the slag-heaps of our troubles and sorrows,
Sweep away, thunder-rain, the slime from our valleys,
And let our streets, our home, our visions
Be cleansed and be shining when the evening comes
With its rainbow arching the smiling uplands,
With its glittering trees and laughing flowers,
And its mountains bright with the setting sun.

44

You men of Gwent and Gwalia
From Neath to Ebbw Vale,
Sing us a song of triumph
Out of a Celtic tale.

Sing to the crowded valleys
Anthems of heaven and earth,
Stir the blood within us
And flood our hearts with mirth.

You tenors from Treorchy,
Basses from Abercwmboi,
Sing to the hills and valleys,
Rouse all the people to joy.

45

Now on your quick allotment
Plant your dream beyond disaster,
Nourish roots to split the strata
Of death. Train the wrist for harvest
And rouse the scarlet rose from clay,
Keeping man's eye on corn and flesh
That he shall murmur tonight
And every night among the secret forest
Of faith and fortitude and truth,
And wage an everlasting war
On the swollen roots of vulgarity.

46

' What are you doing, young man, alone
In the grass on the mountain side ? '
I'm reading a bit of Shakespeare
Who writes of love and pride.

' O why do you waste your time, young man,
Alone on the mountain side ? '
I want to go down to the valley some day
To sing of love and pride.

' Do you think to be great some day, young man,
From your dreams on the mountain side ? '
I only desire that the land of my birth
Breed in me love and pride.

[*The Angry Summer*

47

In Capel Hebron the choirs are singing,
And Martha and Jane and Hywel and Emrys
Are lost in the rapture of anthem and chorus
And the walls of the chapel are shaking with song,
And wave after wave of music crashes
Over the maddened multitude.
Chorus of Handel, mighty and glorious,
Rolls and reverberates again and again,
Tearing the barriers and bastions asunder,
Shaking the heart and the depths of the soul.
O spirit of music and wonder and passion
Flood with thy rapture our derelict valleys,
And give unto men the motive to action,
The impulse to build what is worthy of man.

48

The telephones are ringing
And treachery's in the air.
The sleek one,
The expert at compromise
Is bowing in Whitehall.
And lackey to fox to parrot cries :
' The nation must be saved '.
What is the nation, gentlemen,
Who are the nation, my lords ?
The sleek one,
The expert at compromise,
Is chattering in Whitehall.
The men who have made this nation,

Who have made her gross in wealth,
The men who have given their flesh and blood
From century to century,
They do not scream and panic,
They do not cringe and whine,
They do not shudder in the hour of crisis.
It is the robber and the gambler and the parasite
Who yell when the hour of reckoning comes.
But the sleek one,
The expert at compromise,
Is signing in Whitehall.
The buying and selling is over,
The treachery sealed, and called
A national triumph ;
And this Friday goes down to history
Yellow, and edged with black.

49

Your fathers fought and suffered
And died for their daily bread,
And on the sides of your mountains
Sleep the heroic dead.

Bugles will not wake them
From the eternal night,
But you will be sons of theirs,
Keeping their torches bright.

[The Angry Summer

50

The summer wanes, and the wine of words
Departs with the departing birds.
The roses are withering one by one
And the lesser grasses grow sick of the sun,
The mountain tops are brown and bare
And listless grows the secret hare.
Mother to mother begins to sigh
And slander is added to brazen lie
In many a distant seaside town
Where tempers go up when profits go down.
And here and there a traitor crawls
Back to the enemy's coloured walls
Where food is rich and drink is free
To those who trade in treachery.
But the battle's end is not defeat
To that dream that guided the broken feet
And roused to beauty and to pride
Toiler and toiler, side by side,
Whose faith and courage shall be told
In blaze of scarlet and of gold.

DAVID ALLEN EVANS, R.A.F.

Lower him gently into his grave,
One of the gentle, one of the brave,
Lower him gently, let him lie
Under his native earth and sky.

So ends his youth upon the earth,
His twenty years of love and mirth,
And is our dream a dream in vain
That we shall meet with him again ?

He will forget our night and day
And the blood of battles far away,
He will forget our pain and tears
And our dark tumultuous years.

But shall the deeper truths be told
Beyond the waters black and cold,
Or is our dream a dream in vain
That we shall meet with him again ?

Lower him gently, let him be
Asleep unto eternity,
Lower him gently, let him lie
Under his native earth and sky.

Treorchy, December 21, 1943

SNOWFLAKE

From wandering in Worcester,
  In Merthyr, and in Bow,
This is the truth I gather,
  As naked as the snow :

The cur shall be in clover,
  The poet in the sleet,
Till Christ comes into Dover
  With fire at His feet.

THE INNER LIGHT

Unto the promised haven
The tribes of Israel came,
Weary and thirsty and angry
And Moses bore the blame.

And they laid him low in Moab
And mourned him thirty days,
But did they weep for Moses
Or for his Master's ways ?

Deep are the springs of sorrow,
Too deep for brain to scan,
And the inner light is a dim one
From Dublin unto Dan.

DEFIANCE

I showed my teeth to the London moon
And said, ' You shall not charm to-night.
I shall not be the slave of moonlit streams,
And midnight moors, and cold black pines,
And long blue ridges in the West.
There is a splendour must be left unsaid—
You shall not touch my heart to-night.
There is a magic that I know too well,
A loveliness beyond all sighing and all art,
And I will be no neophyte this hour.
Die, moon, you ravisher of boys !
There are goats and peacocks on the misty lawns.
And bearded musicians on the lake,
And smitten daughters at the harbour quay,
And dark, game women on the Holborn kerb,
And spoils enough for you to-night.
Die, moon, you vixen of the South !'
And I drew the mediaeval curtain
Sharp across the glass, and killed the moon.

GENUINE CYNIC

The moon is a genuine cynic
Who watches the poets die,
And statesmen in lilac bathrooms
And priests who study to sigh,
And she has smiled and listened
Behind the summer oak
At dirty little orators
Who fool the empty folk.

But she has no silver daughters
Nor sons to share her lore
Only the servile moaning tides
Dragged to the murdering shore,
And so her wondrous wisdom
Is locked in a casket of smiles,
And she has a sure memory
And a mastery of styles.

RUIN

And now the crippled cowman calls
Across the ruins in the rain :
' Beware the dagger in the dusk,
The steel that seeks the ageing brain.'

The snake lies low behind the thorn
And grins on rural innocence,
The river grumbles in the mist
And bailiffs count the shabby pence.

Tomorrow death shall be desired
In lofts and cellars damp with dreams,
And the sourest servant hang
Head down along eternal beams.

ULTIMATE AUTUMN

One shall stammer of decay
And one shall bleed the harvest home
And one shall cry along the sea
And one deny the mountain tomb.

And no desire shall there be,
No promise and no tryst,
And one who slaughtered shall acclaim
A grimmer ghost of Christ.

And in the ultimate autumn
The idiot and the horse
Shall sleep and dream for ever
Of man and all his wars.

PERMANENCE

The road bends out of the valley town
And climbs the brown hill
Where the stonechat and the summer furze
Shall recall for the aged man
The summer his youth could not recall,
The summer behind the golden tree,
And a girl in a great room playing,
Her fingers like lilies laughing
On the fringe of the noonday sky.

Where this road bends this minute, now,
The tall tree nods to the lorry and the grocer's car,
And this is a Friday evening aware of eternity,
A thought that rests on a stone,
And there are words forgotten that strive
To create a poem of children gathering may
In a far place
Where this road bends this minute, now,
Where this road bends and is bright for ever.

Whitsun, 1944

I WAS BORN IN RHYMNEY

I was born in Rhymney
To a miner and his wife—
On a January morning
I was pulled into this Life.

Among Anglicans and Baptists
And Methodists I grew,
And my childhood had to chew and chance
The creeds of such a crew.

I went to church and chapel
Ere I could understand
That Apollo rules the heavens
And Mammon rules the land.

And I woke on many mornings
In a little oblong room,
And saw the frown of Spurgeon :
' Beware, my boy, of doom.'

And there was the family Bible
Beneath a vase of flowers,
With pictures of the Holy Land
That enchanted me for hours.

And there was my Uncle Edward,
Solemn and stern and grey,
A Calvinistic Methodist
Who made me kneel and pray.

He would carry me on his shoulders
When I was six or seven
And tell me of the golden days
When chariots flew to heaven.

He was furious against Pharaoh
And scornful about Eve,
But his pathos about Joseph
Could always make me grieve.

He knew the tribes and customs
And the apt geography
Of Jerusalem and Jericho
And the hills of Galilee.

And Moses was his hero
And Jehovah was his God.
And his stories were as magical
As Aaron's magic rod.

But sometimes from the Bible
He would turn to politics
And tell of Gladstone's glory
And Disraeli's little tricks.

But even William Ewart Gladstone
Of beloved memory
Would fade and be forgotten
When it came to D.L.G.

The little Celt from Criccieth,
The Liberal on fire,
He was the modern Merlin
And Moses and Isaiah !

The ghost of Uncle Edward
In a solemn bowler hat,
Does it haunt the plains of Moab
Or the slopes of Ararat ?

Or lurks it in the Gateway,
Where Peter holds the key,
To welcome on the harp strings
The ghost of D.L.G. ?

I lost my native language
For the one the Saxon spake
By going to school by order
For education's sake.

I learnt the use of decimals,
And where to place the dot,
Four or five lines from Shakespeare
And twelve from Walter Scott.

I learnt a little grammar,
And some geography,
Was frightened of perspective,
And detested poetry.

In a land of narrow valleys,
And solemn Sabbath Days,
And collieries and choirs,
I learnt my people's ways.

I looked on local deacons
With not a little awe,
I waved a penny Union Jack
When Asquith went to war.

I pinned my faith in Kitchener
And later in Haig and Foch,
And pitied little Belgium
And cursed the bloody Boche.

We warred along the hillsides
And volleyed sticks and stones,
And sometimes smashed the windows
Of Mrs. Hughes and Jones.

We stood in queues for apples,
For paraffin, and jam,
And were told to spit on Lenin,
And honour Uncle Sam.

But often in the evenings
When all the stars were out
We played beneath the lamp-post
And did not stop to doubt

That the world was made for children
Early on Christmas Day
By a jolly old whiskered Josser
In a mansion far away.

And there were the hours for Chaplin,
Pearl White, and Buffalo Bill,
And the hours for nests and whinberries
High on the summer hill.

And O the hour of lilac
And a leopard in the sky,
And the heart of childhood singing
A song that cannot die !

I learnt of Saul and Jesus
In the little Sunday School,
And later learnt to muse and doubt
By some lonely mountain pool.

I saw that creeds could comfort
And hypocrisy console
But in my blood were battles
No Bible could control.

And I praised the unknown Artist
Of crag and fern and stream
For the sunshine on the mountains
And the wonder of a dream.

127

Start down mine.

On one February morning,
Unwillingly I went
To crawl in moleskin trousers
Beneath the rocks of Gwent.

And a chubby little collier
Grew fat on sweat and dust,
And listened to heated arguments
On God and Marx and lust.

For seven years among the colliers
I learnt to laugh and curse,
When times were fairly prosperous
And when they were ten times worse.

And I loved and loved the mountains
Against the cloudy sky,
The sidings, and the slag-heaps
That sometimes hurt the eye.

MacDonald was my hero,
The man who seemed inspired,
The leader with a vision,
Whose soul could not be hired !

I quoted from his speeches
In the coalface to my friends—
But I lived to see him selling
Great dreams for little ends.

And there were strikes and lock-outs
And meetings in the Square,
When Cook and Smith and Bevan
Electrified the air.

But the greatest of our battles
We lost in '26
Through treachery and lying,
And Baldwin's box of tricks.

I began to read from Shelley
In afternoons in May,
And to muse upon the misery
Of unemployment pay.

I stood in queues for hours
Outside the drab Exchange,
With my hands deep in my pockets
In a suit I could not change.

I stood before Tribunals
And smothered all my pride,
And bowed to my inferiors,
And raged with my soul outside.

And I walked my native hillsides
In sunshine and in rain,
And learnt the poet's language
To ease me of my pain.

With Wordsworth and with Shelley
I scribbled out my dreams,
Sometimes among the slag-heaps,
Sometimes by mountain streams.

O I shook hands with Shelley
Among the moonlit fern,
And he smiled, and slowly pointed
To the heart that would not burn.

And I discovered Milton
In a shabby little room
Where I spent six summer evenings
In most luxurious gloom.

I met Macbeth and Lear,
And Falstaff full of wine,
And I went one day to Stratford
To tread on ground divine.

And I toiled through dismal evenings
With algebraical signs,
With Euclid and Pythagoras
And all their points and lines.

Sometimes there came triumph
But sometimes came despair,
And I would fling all books aside
And drink the midnight air.

And there were dark and bitter mornings
When the streets like coffins lay
Between the winter mountains,
Long and bleak and grey.

But season followed season
And beauty never died
And there were days and hours
Of hope and faith and pride.

In springtime I went roaming
Along the Severn Sea,
Rejoicing in the tempest
And its savage ecstasy.

And there were summer evenings
By Taf, and Usk, and Wye,
When the land was bright with colour
Beneath a quiet sky.

But always home to Rhymney
From wandering I came,
Back to the long and lonely
Self-tuition game,

Back to Euclid's problems,
And algebraical signs,
And the routes of trade and commerce,
And Caesar's battle lines,

Back to the lonely evenings
Of triumph and despair
In a little room in Rhymney
With a hint of mountain air.

O days I shall remember
Until I drop and die !—
Youth's bitter sweet progression
Beneath a Rhymney sky.

At last I went to college,
To the city on the Trent,
In the land of D. H. Lawrence
And his savage Testament.

And history and poetry
Filled all my days and nights,
And in the streets of Nottingham
I harnessed my delights.

I loved the leafy villages
Along the winding Trent,
And sometimes sighed at sunset
For the darker hills of Gwent.

And the churches of East Anglia
Delighted heart and eye,
The little steepled churches
Against the boundless sky.

And lecture followed lecture
In the college by the lake,
And some were sweet to swallow,
And some were hard to take.

I read from Keats and Lawrence,
And Eliot, Shaw, and Yeats,
And the ' History of Europe
With diagrams and dates '.

I went to Sherwood Forest
To look for Robin Hood,
But little tawdry villas
Were where the oaks once stood.

And I heard the ghost of Lawrence
Raging in the night
Against the thumbs of Progress
That botched the land with blight.

And season followed season
And beauty never died,
And I left the land of Trent again
To roam by Rhymney's side,

By the narrow Rhymney River
That erratically flows
Among the furnace ruins
Where the sullen thistle blows.

Then I tried for posts in Yorkshire,
In Staffordshire and Kent,
For hopeless was the striving
For any post in Gwent.

I wrote out testimonials
Till my hands began to cry
That the world was full of jackals
And beasts of smaller fry.

At last, at last, in London
On one November day,
I began to earn my living,
To weave my words for pay.

At last I walked in London,
In park and square and street,
In bright and shady London
Where all the nations meet.

At last I lived in London
And saw the sun go down
Behind the mists of Richmond
And the smoke of Camden Town.

I watched the King of England
Go riding with his queen,
I watched the cats steal sausage
From stalls in Bethnal Green.

I tried the air of Hampstead,
I tried the brew of Bow,
I tried the cake of Kensington
And the supper of Soho.

I rode in trams and taxis
And tried the social round,
And hurried home to Highgate
On the London Underground.

In little rooms in London
The poetry of Yeats
Was my fire and my fountain—
And the fury of my mates.

I found cherries in Jane Austen
And grapes in Hemingway,
And truth more strange than fiction
In the streets of Holloway.

And da Vinci and El Greco
And Turner and Cézanne,
They proved to me the splendour
And divinity of man.

I gazed at stones from Hellas,
And heard imagined trees
Echo across the ages
The words of Sophocles.

And often of a Sunday
I hailed the highest art,
The cataracts and gardens
Of Wagner and Mozart.

I studied Marx and Engels,
And put Berkeley's theme aside,
And listened to the orators
Who yelled and cooed and cried.

O the orators, the orators,
On boxes in the parks,
They judge the Day of Judgment
And award Jehovah marks.

O the orators, the orators,
When shall their voices die ?
When London is a soap-box
With its bottom to the sky.

In many a public library
I watched the strong men sleep,
And virgins reading volumes
Which made their blushes deep.

Sometimes I watched the Commons
From the narrow galleries,
My left eye on the Premier,
My right on the Welsh M.P.s.

In Christopher Wren's Cathedral
I heard Dean Inge lament
The lack of care in breeding
From Caithness down to Kent.

And once in the ancient Abbey
I heard Thomas Hardy sigh :
' O why must a Wessex pagan
Here uneasily lie ? '

To Castle Street Baptist Chapel
Like the prodigal son I went
To hear the hymns of childhood
And dream of a boy in Gwent,

To dream of far-off Sundays
When for me the sun would shine
On the broken hills of Rhymney
And the palms of Palestine.

With Tory and with Communist,
With atheist and priest,
I talked and laughed and quarrelled
Till light lit up the east.

The colonel and his nonsense,
The busman and his cheek,
I liked them all in London
For seven days a week.

O sometimes I was merry
In Bloomsbury and Kew,
When fools denied their folly
And swore that pink was blue.

And sometimes I lounged sadly
By the River in the night
And watched a body diving
And passing out of sight.

When the stars were over London
And lights lit up the Town,
I banished melancholy
And kept the critic down.

When the moon was bright on Eros
And the cars went round and round,
The whores arrived from Babylon
By the London Underground.

O I stood in Piccadilly
And sat in Leicester Square,
And mused on satin and sewerage
And lice and laissez-faire.

I saw some royal weddings
And a Silver Jubilee,
And a coloured Coronation,
And a King who crossed the sea.

In springtime to the shires
I went happy and alone,
And entered great cathedrals
To worship glass and stone.

I had holidays in Eire
Where the angels drink and dance,
And with a Tam from Ayrshire
I roamed the South of France.

For week-ends in the winter
When cash was pretty free,
I went to stay in Hastings
To argue by the sea.

For Sussex in the winter
Was dearer to me
Than Sussex full of trippers
Beside the summer sea.

In the wreck of Epping Forest
I listened as I lay
To the language of the Ghetto
Behind a hedge of May.

And in the outer suburbs
I heard in the evening rain
The cry of Freud the prophet
On love and guilt and pain.

And on the roads arterial,
When London died away,
The poets of the Thirties
Were singing of decay.

I saw the placards screaming
About Hitler and his crimes,
Especially on Saturdays—
That happened many times.

And I saw folk digging trenches
In 1938,
In the dismal autumn drizzle
When all things seemed too late.

And Chamberlain went to Munich,
An umbrella at his side,
And London lost her laughter
And almost lost her pride.

I saw the crowds parading
And heard the angry cries
Around the dusty monuments
That gazed with frozen eyes.

The lands were full of fear,
And Hitler full of scorn,
And London full of critics
Whose nerves were badly torn.

And crisis followed crisis
Until at last the line
Of battle roared to fire
In 1939.

And then evacuation,
And London under fire,
And London in the distance,
The city of desire.

And the world is black with battle
In 1943,
And the hymn of hate triumphant
And loud from sea to sea.

And in this time of tumult
I can only hope and cry
That season shall follow season
And beauty shall not die.

Autumn, 1943

III Glory out of Chaos

TONYPANDY

Working class
struggle
W. C. Hero.

I

Dai bach, Dai bach, with your woollen muffler
Tight around your stout dark neck,
Why do you seem so sad and lonely
There at the corner of Pandy Square,
Now in this moist grey hour of twilight
And colourless streets and long black hills?
Are your eyes on those birds that have strayed from the sea,
Those few smooth gulls up from the Severn,
Floating and crying below the clouds,
Complaining and floating above the valley-sides?
Do the sea-birds awaken old sorrows at dusk
There at the corner of Pandy Square,
As they circle and sigh above the slag-heaps
And the narrow brown river trickling
Between the crooked streets and the colliery sidings?
Are they as poems from the Severn Sea,
Sad little lyrics borne on the dusk wind
Over the coastal plain and over the valleys
Up to the mountains and mists of Glamorgan,
Haunting the twilight, haunting the heart?
Or do they remind you, David, you son of Tonypandy,
Of summer afternoons on holiday beaches,
And cheap excursions to Weston-super-Mare,
With the steamer chuff-chuff-chuffing across the Channel
And the Flatholm in the distance, and the sunshine
Radiant over the Somerset cliffs and gardens,
And your Martha, with her mouth wide open,

Leaning against you on the crowded deck,
And the Sunday School parties all around you
Sweating with singing the sad, sad hymns ?
And O it was sweet in the evening, Dai,
After the bathing and the dancing and the pastries and the
      ice-cream,
And the gardens of roses behind the coloured town,
And the nut-brown ale in the pub by the pier,
Ay, it was sweet upon the evening waters
To watch the sun go down in scarlet
Behind the far promontory, and gaze upon
The velvet undulations of the sea,
And sweet it was to dream, Dai bach,
With Martha warm and fragrant, close against you,
Martha from Treorchy nestled in your arms,
Sweet it was to coo of love and summer
To the rhythm and the moaning of the darkening sea,
And the pleasure-boat chuff-chuff-chuffing homewards
Towards the lights of Cardiff in the bluish distance,
And the waiting quays and the quayside station,
With your Day Excursion tickets sticky in your hands.
Or do I dream that you dream like this
There as you stand in the dreary dusk,
There at the corner of Pandy Square ?

II

When you were young, Dai, when you were young !
The Saturday mornings of childhood
With childish dreams and adventures
Among the black tips by the river,
And the rough grass and the nettles
Behind the colliery yard, the stone-throwing
Battles between the ragged boys,
The fascination of the railway cutting
On dusty summer afternoons,
And the winter night and its street-lamps
And the first pranks of love,
And the deep warm sleep
In grandmother's chapel pew
On stodgy Sunday evenings,
And the buttercup-field you sometimes noticed
Behind the farthest street, the magical field
That only the heart could see,
The heart and rarely the boyish eye,
And the pride you had in your father's
Loins and shoulders when he bent
Between the tub and the fire,
And the days you counted, counted, counted,
Before you should work in the mine.
You never, never cursed your luck
Or desired to see another town or valley,

146   [*Tonypandy*

Or know any other men and women
Than those of the streets around
The street where you were born.
Your world was narrow and magical
And dear and dirty and brave
When you were young, Dai, when you were young !

III

The dusk deepens into the autumn night,
The cold drizzle spreads across the valleys,
The rubbish heaps are lost among the mists,
And where will you go for the evening, Dai,
For the evening in Tonypandy ?
Will you count your coppers and join
The cinema queue where the tired women
Huddle like sheep, and comfort one another
With signs and sentimental phrases,
And where some folk blame the local councillors
For all the evils of the day and night ?
O in the little queue, what tales are told
When we have shuffled off the burdens of the day—
What rancour, what compassion, what relief !
Or perhaps you will go to the prayer meeting down the chapel,
Where the newest member can pray for an hour without
    stopping,

The one converted at the last Big Meeting.
Or will you go to the pub at the corner
Where tongues come loose and hearts grow soft,
Where politics are so easy to understand,
Where the Irish labourer explains the constitution of de Valera,
And the Tory Working Man snarls behind his beer
At those who do not worship Winston Churchill,
And those who vaguely praise the Beveridge Report.
Or perhaps you will go back to your fireside this evening
And talk with your Martha of the children abroad,
The son out in Italy, the quick-tongued Ifor,
And the young quiet Emrys in the R.A.F.,
And Mair, with her roses and her laughing eyes,
So sprightly in her khaki uniform ;
And you will be proud and you will be sad,
And you will be brave for Martha's sake,
And you will be Dai the great of heart.

IV

So much you have given, so little received,
O Dai, you miner of Tonypandy !
And ' blessed it is to give ' the Bible says—
My God, then you ought to be an angel,
An angel in the Garden of Empire,
With wings of Red, White and Blue !

But to-night as you sit by your kitchen fire
You know in your heart how your life has been
    botched,
Been robbed of peace and grace and beauty,
Of leisure to dream and build and create,
Not the leisure of the shabby witless idler,
But the leisure that burgeons with proud achievement,
The leisure that marks an awakened nation
Exultantly singing the joy of the earth.
How silently and subtly and surely the chains
Have bound the mind and the body
To the status quo of the iron jungle !
Men have gone down unknown through the ages,
Down to the shame that is deeper than death,
Darkness behind them, darkness before them,
Ravaged by hunger to desperation
And goaded and whipped and tortured
For the sake of a pampered despotic few.
And here in your home in Tonypandy,
Tonight by this fire that flickers and dies,
You know that these words are not figures of fancy,
You know that they echo the thoughts in your heart.

V

Dai in his bed, and Tonypandy
Silent under the silent stars,
Silent and black and cold beneath the autumn night,
The night so full of mystery and memory,
The night of stars above the streets of Tonypandy ;
And you shall listen to the footsteps crossing Pandy Square,
The echoes of the footsteps silenced long ago,
Dear, dogged footsteps marching to the sound of drum and
    fife,
Footsteps whose echoes were heard across the mountains,
Footsteps of toilers and rebels and dreamers,
And the echoes of bullets and galloping horses
And curses and desperate rallying calls.
And older far than all those echoes
You hear the battle cries of Celtic kings
And bearded chieftains in the virgin valleys
Riding in scarlet and yellow to the castles by the Severn Sea.
And the skies that look down to-night and to-morrow
On slag-heaps and hovels and little bowler-hatted deacons,
On square grey chapels and gasometers and pubs,
Once saw Cadwgan and his shining battle-axe
Rallying his warriors among the summer mountains,
And Owain Glyndwr sweeping southward to the feudal
    coast,
With colour and with music and with pride
And Dai's forefathers roused by song and banner,
Alive to the passionate lore of Gwalia,

Crowding and flocking and roaring to battle
Between the hills and the forests and the Severn Sea,
Martyrs to freedom and the Celtic dream.
And will that dream disturb one sleeping youth to-night
Beneath the roofs, among the streets of Tonypandy ?
And shall the Future mock our simple, simple faith
In the Progress that has scorned the native culture,
The legend and the vision and the dream,
And a people that has nigh lost its history and language
To serve with blood and flesh the maw of Mammon ?
O singers, singers in a thousand years to be,
Who shall sing of joys our richest hearts can never conceive,
Forget not the dreams of the few who dream to-night
Among the rubbish heaps of 1944 !
And forgive and pity and remember those
Whose souls were narrowed by the joyless day,
The lack of bread, the sordid strife,
The penury inherited from father to son to son,
And men in chains who did not feel the chains.
And singers, singers, in a distant golden time to be,
Remember a little of Dai and Tonypandy,
Dai and his Martha and his fireside,
Dai and his lamp in the depths of the earth,
Dai and his careless lilting tongue.
Dai and his heart of gold.

Tonypandy]

VI

And meanwhile, Dai, with your woollen muffler
Tight around your pit-scarred neck,
Remind us of the gratitude we owe you,
We who so easily pass you by.

Remind us of your long endurance,
Those bitter battles the sun has never seen,
And remind us of the struggles you have waged
Against the crude philosophy of greed.

And remind all who strut with noses high in the air,
How the proudest of nations would falter without you,
And remind us when we lie on fireside cushions
Of the blood that is burnt within the flame.

And remind us when we kneel to the unknown God
And turn and cry to the cold infinite heavens,
Remind us of the toil of the blistered hands
And the courage and the comradeship of men.

[Tonypandy

IN GARDENS IN THE RHONDDA

In gardens in the Rhondda
  The daffodils dance and shine
When tired men trudge homeward
  From factory and mine.

The daffodils dance in gardens
  Behind the grim brown row
Built among the slagheaps
  In a hurry long ago.

They dance as though in passion
  To shame and to indict
The brutes who built so basely
  In the long Victorian night.

TIGER BAY

I watched the coloured seamen in the morning mist,
Slouching along the damp brown street,
Cursing and laughing in the dismal dawn.
The sea had grumbled through the night,
Small yellow lights had flickered far and near,
Huge chains clattered on the ice-cold quays,
And daylight had seemed a hundred years away . . .
But slowly the long cold night retreated
Behind the cranes and masts and funnels,
The sea-signals wailed beyond the harbour
And seabirds came suddenly out of the mist.
And six coloured seamen came slouching along
With the laughter of the Levant in their eyes
And contempt in their tapering hands.
Their coffee was waiting in some smoke-laden den,
With smooth yellow dice on the unswept table,
And behind the dirty green window
No lazy dream of Africa or Arabia or India,
Nor any dreary dockland morning,
Would mar one minute for them.

THE WIRRAL

So here is the Wirral, flat and moist and grey,
With cattle half asleep in the evening drizzle,
And solitary sportsmen in tweeds
Walking to small untidy stations,
Sniffing the salt as they go.

Wherever I walk on the Wirral, my mind
Is dominated by Liverpool,
A huge black cube on the mental map,
Even the small cool flowers of the marshland
Tremble in the invisible shadow of Liverpool.

Now day dies, and over the estuary
The sharp lights twinkle, the wind blows
Fresher over the mud flats,
Across the Mersey the sirens wail,
And mighty in the darkening twilight
Looms Liverpool, pretending to be respectable,
Always stammering of her efficiency,
And always unaware of her shoddiness.
Who shall not pay in the Central Market
A shilling for a broken heart?

Come again morning, cool grey morning,
Over the broad brown Mersey,
And I will walk out to praise in silence
The fascinating flatness of the Wirral,
And admire the cattle in the moist green meadow,
The cattle that do not love or fear the distant cathedral,
That look at the angler and his tackle
With soft uncritical eyes.

LONDON WELSH

We have scratched our names in the London dust,
Sung sometimes like the Jews of Babylon
Under the dusty trees of Hyde Park Corner,
Almost believing in a Jesus of Cardigan
Or a Moses on the mountains of Merioneth ;
We have dreamed by the Thames of Towy and Dee,
And whistled in dairy shops in the morning,
Whistled of Harlech and Aberdovey.
We have grown sentimental in London
Over things that we smiled at in Wales.
Sometimes in Woolwich we have seen the mining valleys
More beautiful than we ever saw them with our eyes.
We have carried our accents into Westminster
As soldiers carry rifles into the wars ;
We have carried our idioms into Piccadilly,
Food for the critics on Saturday night.
We have played dominoes in Lambeth with Alfred the Great,
And lifted a glass with Henry VIII
In the tavern under the railway bridge
On Friday nights in winter ;
And we have argued with Chaucer down the Old Kent
    Road
On the englynion of the Eisteddfod.
We have also shivered by the Thames in the night
And known that the frost has no racial distinctions.

IN HATTON GARDEN

I walked through Hatton Garden
    And gazed to left and right,
And wondered if the merchants
    Slept soundly in the night.

O diamonds and rubies
    Are things I cannot buy,
And yet in Hatton Garden
    I found no cause to sigh.

For the stones I love and treasure,
    No man will work them ill,
The grass grows wild around them
    For ever on Rhymney Hill.

THE SOCIALIST VICTORY

Blow on your morning bugles,
 Sons of the morning hills,
Stand on the graves of your fathers,
 See that your day fulfils
All that they bled and died for
 Who dreamed their blood should bring
A greater, prouder nation
 And a greater song to sing.

Blow on your morning bugles,
 Sons of the morning hills,
Awaken the slumbering warriors,
 Awaken the strength that wills
A world of lovelier nations
 And a surer ecstasy.
Blow on your morning bugles
 And shake the morning sea.

A CAROL FOR THE COALFIELD

From the moors of Blaen Rhymni down to the leaning wall
Of Caerphilly Castle you shall hear the same accents
Of sorrow and mirth and pride, and a vague belief
That the future shall be greater than the past.

The man in the Rhondda Valley and the man in Abertillery
Have shared the same years, the same days of hope and desolation,
And in Ogmore Vale and in Ammanford both old and young
    dream
That the future shall be greater than the past.

On the ragged hills and by the shallow polluted rivers,
The pious young man and the old rascal of many sins,
The idealists and the wasters, all sometimes believe and say
That the future shall be greater than the past.

Mothers praying for sons away in the wars, and mothers waiting
On doorsteps and by firesides for men coming home from the
    pits,
And the old folk bent and scarred with years of toil, all sometimes
    hope
That the future shall be greater than the past.

Last night the moon was full above the slag heaps and the
    grave-yards
And the towns among the hills, and a man arose from his dream
And cried out : Let this day be sufficient, and worthy of my
    people
And let the night winds go on wailing of the future and the past.
1945

IN DYFED

Beyond the silver harbours where the chronicles were told
The great white birds of memory rise and whirl and call,
And the cool night comes softly from the western sea,
The night and its memory of broken kings,
Of disastrous days and towers fallen,
And the bloodstained corn beaten back into the dust,
And the dim saint journeying
Among the hovels, the caves by the pagan seas,
The dimmest of saints in the dusk
Seeing lions in the purple ruins at the ends of the earth
Roaring at the vast deaf sea.
For all our history is the echoing of echoes
In desolate places by desolate shores,
The frenzy of the fool, the sigh of the sage,
And Babylon daring Orion into the labyrinths of lust.
And so you shall recall the wild legends of this land
Where laughter was silenced on a summer day
And shadows fell upon the grassless rocks,
And ghost with ghost knelt down and pondered on
The melancholy glory born of human love
And the great love that sorrow breeds again.

THE DREAM CITY

(From the Welsh of Sir John Morris Jones)

O linger here a while, my love,
   And put thy hand in mine,
And gaze across the waters where
   That city seems divine.

A mist purpureal lightly lies
   Around her as a veil,
She stands afar as though she were
   One in a fairy tale.

As fair and transient is the life
   I lead beside the sea,
And o'er it all a wondrous charm
   Was cast my love, by thee.

A life ethereal as a dream
   Is granted unto me ;
By summer waters do I dwell
   On the shores of Gramarye.

ARFON

All this rugged land is sacred
And its glory shall not die,
Where the mountains meet the Menai,
Where Eryri cleaves the sky.

Here of old the harp and bugle
Stirred the fettered to be free,
And the wild winds waved the banners
That led to pride and liberty.

Here of old the blazing torches
Thrilled the heart and thrilled the eye,
Where the mountains meet the Menai,
Where Eryri cleaves the sky.

Here, this eve, the shores are quiet
And all Arfon seems at rest,
And we with dreams can but remember
Those whose days with deeds were blest.

Still those warriors wage *our* battles
And their voices shall not die
Where the mountains meet the Menai,
Where Eryri cleaves the sky.

Still a golden language triumphs
On these mountains by the sea,
And I heard a child this morning
Sing of Glyndwrs yet to be.
1950

SAUNDERS LEWIS

Though some may cavil at his creed
 And others mock his Celtic ire,
No Welshman loyal to his breed
 Forgets this prophet dared the fire,
And roused his land by word and deed
 Against Philistia and her mire.

DYLAN THOMAS

He saw the sun play ball in Swansea Bay,
He heard the moon crack jokes above the new-mown hay,
And stars and trees and winds to him would sing and say :
Carve words like jewels for a summer day.

1946

DOWLAIS TOP

What is there here at Dowlais Top to please a poet's eye ?
What is there here but ragged earth against a ragged sky,
A bleak discoloured broken land where only the strayed sheep
        cry ?

So bleak and grim, a waste of stone, rough grass, and weed and
        slag,
And shabby Dowlais down below, where live the sage and wag,
And miles around the great bare hills, the land of Mog and Mag !

And yet to here my heart returns when softer landscapes cloy,
For here I sang my secret song, my silent psalm of joy,
On the day I felt a poet born within the dreaming boy.

For here I found the soul could sing whate'er the eye could see,
Could sing about the beauty lost and the beauty yet to be,
And probe to the impassioned thought that is the root of poetry.

1951

The bleak pollutant. Landscape, gave him his inspiration.

LAND OF MY MOTHERS

Land of my mothers, how shall my brothers praise you?
With timbrels or rattles or tins?
With fire.
How shall we praise you on the banks of the rhymneying waters,
On the smoky shores and the glittering shores of Glamorgan,
On wet mornings in the bare fields behind the Newport docks,
On fine evenings when lovers walk by Bedwellty Church,
When the cuckoo calls to miners coming home to Rhymney
    Bridge,
When the wild rose defies the Industrial Revolution
And when the dear old drunken lady sings of Jesus and a little
    shilling.

Come down, O girls of song, to the bank of the coal canal
At twilight, at twilight
When mongrels fight
And long rats bite
Under the shadows of pit-head light,
And dance, you daughters of Gwenllian,
Dance in the dust in the lust of delight.

And you who have prayed in golden pastures
And oiled the wheels of the Western Tradition
And trod where bards have danced to church,
Pay a penny for this fragment of a burning torch.
It will never go out.

It will gather unto itself all the fires
That blaze between the heavens above and the earth beneath
Until the flame shall frighten each mud-hearted hypocrite
And scatter the beetles fattened on the cream of corruption,
The beetles that riddle the ramparts of Man.

Pay a penny for my singing torch,
O my sisters, my brothers of the land of my mothers,
The land of our fathers, our troubles, our dreams,
The land of Llewellyn and Shoni bach Shinkin,
The land of the sermons that pebble the streams,
The land of the englyn and Crawshay's old engine,
The land that is sometimes as proud as she seems.

And sons of the mountains and sons of the valleys
O lift up your hearts, and then
Lift up your feet.

MISTS UPON THE SEA

I love light mists upon the sea
When I am musing on a shore,
And listening to eternity ;

When I am musing on a shore,
When light's last streaks fade into night,
And one star shines, and far seas roar.

When light's last streaks fade into night,
I think of the frail things forlorn
That only know a dim delight ;

I think of the frail things forlorn
That lie among the mists of eve,
Content that they were only born.

1931 ; revised 1951

LISTENING TO BEETHOVEN

I am listening to Beethoven
And immense promontaries are shining
And gleaming by the vast and glittering seas,
The restless, boundless, wandering seas . . . .
And I know that all the earth is a miracle,
All flesh and all breath and all thought,
A miracle beyond all miracles recorded
In all the strange, fantastic scrolls of ancient time ;
And yet in this hour of mighty dazzling worlds
There is a vision given
Wherein the soul at peace
And in the innermost courts of joy
Can gaze upon the very hands that wrought
Glory out of chaos ;
And the heart of man in this magic hour
Shall listen like a God ecstatic in the heavens
To the first stars singing on the first morning of the
    world.

A YOUNG MAN

O I was young and full of dreams,
A poet by the Syrian streams,
But now I cry on Calvary
Lama, lama, sabachthani ?

I lit a torch and broke the gloom,
And still the Inn denies me room
And here I groan on Calvary
Lama, lama, sabachthani ?

And so I cry on Calvary
Lama, lama, sabachthani ?

22nd August, 1937

BEFORE THE DAWN

He blasted every stone around his tomb
And sang before one cock of spring
Crowed on the Syrian tree.
He sang a dance, he danced a song
Before the world could write his name
In the barbarous cemetery.

He wished the soldiers and the priests
The best of luck when next the moon
Shone down on a desolate Calvary ;
And then, he sang again, and tore
The white and purple robes to rags
And danced the dance of destiny.

RESURRECTION

And I rise, and I remember
    The lads I used to know,
And I must go to greet them
    Ere in the cloud I go.

Though one of them betrayed me,
    And one denied my name,
And the other ten forsook me,
    Yet will I smother blame.

O I will seek and find them
    And talk of what would be
When we were friends together
    On the hills of Galilee.

Though one of them is strangled,
    The other eleven live,
And I will smile upon them
    To show that I forgive.

And I will stand before them
    Till every doubt is dead,
And speak of peaceful pleasures
    Ere thorns were round my head.

And I will talk of troubles
    And joys that used to be
When we were friends together
    On the hills of Galilee.

BIG BROWN BIBLE

Out of the big brown Bible
My fathers took their words,
And flung them in their anger
As stones are flung at birds
That rob the ripening cherries
In warm midsummer days—
And sometimes the words would murder
Or wound in cruel ways.

Out of the big brown Bible
Our speech comes less and less—
We have the blood of our fathers,
We, too, can curse and bless,
We, too, can maim and murder,
And slide from love to hate—
But we do not praise a Jehovah
Whose avenging arm is great.

Out of the big brown Bible,
If we read again, and aright,
Perhaps there may come a language
To banish the darkest night,
To scatter the hosts of hatred
And rally the hosts of love
Till the earth and the sea are singing
And the stars in the heavens above.

BEYOND THE BLACK TIPS

(from a verse play)

The Dreamer from the Mining Town :
> You may smile as the moon smiles, if you will,
> Guardian of the silent gate, for unafraid
> I walk tonight, my body left behind
> In restless sleep upon a toiler's bed,
> And I am the spirit of my midnight dream
> Come out to ease the aching of my heart.

The Guardian of the Gate :
> You've scorned the dust, so trivial and so proud,
> In this horn of the moon and the crowing of the cock
> And perhaps you hope for secrets that the heart,
> The too impetuous heart, desires,
> When earth and sky are loud with lamentation ?
> Or do you come but as a child first comes
> Into the world, unconscious of the accident of life ?

Dreamer :
> I come because my heart has heard a song
> And seeks the words that may the music fit ;
> And the far cockcrow and the light of the moon
> Are only in the shadow of my dream.

Guardian :
> I love a voice that cracks the glass of life
> And makes the whole world dim, most pale and dim
> Against that sudden blaze of light
> That flashes from the mind made swift
> By the purged imagination.

The Guardian and the Dreamer :

>The far cock crows because his lust
>Is lust devoid of crime,
>The round moon rolls because she must
>Serve God's eternal rhyme
>When planets wheel
>And meteors prance
>To the splendour born of fire,
>And the heavens reel
>In a frenzied dance
>To desire beyond desire.

Voices of the Air :

>The Hand that made the heavens
>And ordered night and day,
>Shall wonder add to wonder
>When the heavens have passed away.

>The Hand that fixed the planets
>In numberless array,
>Shall wonder add to wonder
>When the worlds have passed away.

>The Hand that moulded Adam
>Out of a heap of clay,
>Shall wonder add to wonder
>When all flesh has passed away.

The Hand that made the heavens
And ordered night and day,
Shall wonder add to wonder
When the heavens have passed away.

Guardian :

Go, dreamer, back before the night grows grey,
Go back into the world below the hill,
The world of food and clothes, and troubled rest,
And broken hearts, and all the common cares
Of all the common days and common nights ;
Go back before the moon is gone behind
The pit-head stacks and the long crooked streets
Upon the valley sides.
Go back into your mining town,
Go back before the moon is down
And day is come again.

1946

CHRISTMAS EVE 1946

The shepherds watch tonight again
   The star above the byre
Where Mary's child is born again
   Unto the heart's desire.

The angels sing tonight again
   Of God who gives to earth
His gift of love and joy again
   To all who seek his mirth.

The wise men walk tonight again
   To Bethlehem afar
To worship and to praise again
   The babe beneath the star.

And we shall sing tonight again
   The songs of other years,
Until our hearts are young again
   Behind our hidden tears.

24th December, 1946

THE CHRISTMAS TREE

It shone, it sparkled, it was bright
With all the stars of Christmas night,
And every child that came to see
And wonder at that shining tree
Made it more radiant, for those eyes
Lent it the joy of Paradise.

December, 1947

A STAR IN THE EAST

When Christmastide to Rhymney came
   And I was six or seven
I thought the stars in the eastern sky
   Were the brightest stars of heaven.

I chose the star that glittered most
   To the east of Rhymney town
To be the star above the byre
   Where Mary's babe lay down.

And nineteen hundred years would meet
   Beneath a magic light,
And Rhymney share with Bethlehem
   A star on Christmas night.

THE RETIRED ACTOR

Once the crowds applauded me, and now
I will in a quiet room applaud the crowd
And always myself. For the blood of my life
Was applause, applause of the fool and the sage,
Of the mother and child. The theatre shall never be empty,
For in the auditorium the echoes linger
And never completely die away.
Fame is the far-off and never dying legend
Of the artist's pride, and my pride
Is an old romantic ruin, mellow in September's sun.
My Lear shall carry his dead Cordelia to the edge of the world,
My Othello shall curse for ever the midsummer moon,
My Falstaff be merry in ale on my funeral day,
My green Fool fool about with the ashes of my heart.

10th April, 1951

UNDER THE ETHER

White, white walls, and white figures
Moving all around, and a white hand
Approaching the heart, and then a gentle pressure
Behind a small, cool mask on the face ;
And soon the white walls crumbled,
And slowly, slowly the world dissolved
Into space that grew vaster and vaster,
Into space more silent
Than the silence of the earth's most silent hour ;
And then all that was conscious passed
Like a tiny leaf borne on a quiet breeze
Into oblivion . . .

March, 1952

HOSPITAL NURSE

Her art is not the proud to please
Nor is her skill in vain,
For God has given her grace to ease
Humanity in pain.

1952

PSALM

Make us, O Lord, a people fit for poetry,
And grant us clear voices to praise all noble achievement.
Make our guardians wiser than their fathers before them
Who sought the name below the easy jingle
And starved the poet without a name.
Give us fresh eyes to see Thy earth anew,
To see the animal and the grass and the water
As the first man saw them in the dawn.
Grant us, O Lord, Thy benediction
When we are restless and groping in the shadows,
And lead us to the shining mountains.
Make us worthy of the golden chorus
That the sons of God have always yearned to sing.
Make us, O Lord, a people fit for poetry.

INDEX OF TITLES

INDEX OF FIRST LINES

189